THE ILLUSTRATED HISTORY OF
HELICOPTERS

THE ILLUSTRATED HISTORY OF
HELICOPTERS

MICHAEL HEATLEY

Exeter Books

NEW YORK

A Bison Book

CONTENTS

Page 1: Boeing Vertol's CH-47 Chinook has established itself as the greatest twin-rotor helicopter of all time, having served in Vietnam (as shown here), the Falklands and elsewhere.

Pages 2-3: Sikorsky UH-60 Black Hawk unility helicopters of the US Army pictured during desert training in Egypt.

This page: Westland's Westminster was an early variation on the flying crane theme that reached fruition with such types as the Sikorsky S-64 and Mil Mi-10 in the sixties.

Although history traces a consistent process of development from Lilienthal and his gliders to the Wright brothers and their manned flight at Kitty Hawk in 1903, it fails to be as clear-cut about the progress of rotary-wing flight. In some respects this might be considered surprising – the graceful arc of the sycamore seed as it whirls its way to earth seems almost as uncomplicated as nature itself. Yet unraveling the mysteries of rotary-wing flight threw up as many problems as were solved by its pioneers. How to obtain technical control, carry a useful load relative to the weight of the machine, overcome vibration on the ground and defeat the problems of torque were just a few of the obstacles encountered by early experimenters. Little wonder, then, that progress was slow and tortuous, with pioneers pooling their knowledge to defeat the many common problems they found.

When it is considered that fixed wing aircraft were at war in Libya a mere eight years after Kitty Hawk, the thirty-year time span between the first man-carrying helicopter flight in 1907 and the first production machine, the Focke Fa 223 Drache, seems excessive. Yet even this pales into insignificance when compared with the centuries of theorizing on the subject of flight with rotating wings and vanes. Yet whatever ground was lost in the inter-war period was more than regained in the fifties and sixties, decades which saw the helicopter developed in exciting fashion to fulfil many different applications. In addition to using its unique vertical take-off and hovering capabilities for the purposes of air-sea rescue, traffic direction, crop spraying, city center travel and other such socially valuable functions, the vulnerable, slow and noisy helicopter was transformed into a potent weapon of war – the gunship. Armed with rapid-firing miniguns and with a sleek, slim fuselage profile, this was surely the ultimate in military rotorcraft.

The helicopter had already proved its value in the fields of casualty evacuation, anti-submarine warfare and the like. Yet a helicopter with the armament to stop a platoon in its tracks and the maneuverability to use it was something else again. The helicopter had arrived – and military strategists henceforth ignored it at their peril.

All this, of course, was far from the mind of Leonardo da Vinci, the noted Italian artist and scientist who is credited with having designed the first helicopter in 1490. The result of several years' experiment, his model of a helical or lifting screw had lifting surfaces of starched linen – and, he noted, 'if this instrument . . . be turned swiftly, the said screw will make its spiral in the air and it will rise high.' His sketches, however, were not discovered and published until late in the nineteenth century, but nevertheless represented the next step from the 'flying top', observable in the pages of fourth century Chinese literature, that suggest even earlier interest in the principles of vertical flight.

Da Vinci's ideas were elaborated upon by a Frenchman, Paucton, whose Ptérophore of 1768 proposed one screw for vertical and one for horizontal flight. Also from France came the concepts of two men, Launoy and Bienvenu, whose model demonstrated to the Académie des Sciences in 1784 consisted of co-axial rotors at each end of a common shaft, rotated by a bow-string wound around it. Sir George Cayley presented a similar toy to the public in 1809 (although he had in fact developed it some years earlier in 1796) and, in doing so, inspired half a century of such designs.

The latter half of the nineteenth century saw the genesis of many of the concepts later to be employed by the modern man-carrying helicopter: Pomes and de la Pause (1871) proposed a rotor with adjustable pitch, while Achenbach (1874) was the first to record a tail rotor or screw intended to counteract torque. Yet though model helicopters were now flying with elastic propulsion in place of Cayley's bowstring, power was still a problem. Steam, ether vapor, clockwork, man-power and even gunpowder were among the solutions proposed, but it was not until the advent of the internal combustion engine in 1876 that aircraft – whether rotary or fixed-wing – could ever hope to be light enough to sustain flight with a human pilot.

The historic breakthrough at Kitty Hawk in 1903 revitalized the aeronautical sphere – and rotary wing development was no exception. Four years after the Wright brothers' first flights, the man-carrying helicopter finally left mother earth, with two French machines sharing the honors. The four-rotor Breguet-Richet No. 1 lifted its pilot to a height of some two or three feet, but had to be steadied at each of its extremities by ground handlers. It was a mighty machine of cruciform layout, each arm of the cross supporting a four-bladed biplane propeller. Paul Cornu's machine which achieved the first free flight just weeks later in November 1907 was an altogether more workmanlike effort, with twin two-blade rotors fore and aft. Though it only rose for a matter of seconds, Cornu's craft had the stability to write its inventor's name in the record books – and, what was more, required only the 24 horsepower of an Antoinette engine to do so in comparison with its rival's 45 hp motor.

History, then, had finally been made – but if anyone thought the helicopter had overcome all its problems they were mistaken. The hard-won altitude grew foot by painful foot, yet sustained flight seemed as far away as ever; Breguet's second helicopter flew 60 feet but crashed through instability. Russia's Boris Yuriev built a helicopter with a tail rotor in 1912, the same year as J. C. Elle-

Previous page: Frenchman Paul Cornu's machine achieved the first free flight of a rotorcraft in November 1907, some four years after the Wright brothers' fixed-wing breakthrough.

Opposite above: Raoul Pescara's contribution to rotorcraft development was his use of both cyclic and collective pitch for control.

Opposite: The clumsy, cruciform design of the four-rotor Breguet-Richet No. 1 did not prevent it from becoming the first man-carrying helicopter to leave the ground, though it remained tethered during its flight.

hammer (Denmark) produced a co-axial helicopter with a tractor airscrew driven by a 36 hp engine and – more significantly – cyclic (directional) control by means of six vanes adjustable in flight. Yet ultimately the most important character to emerge in these pre-war years was associated with two unsuccessful helicopter designs, choosing temporarily to return to the fixed-wing sphere. His name? Igor Sikorsky.

The acceleration in fixed-wing development promoted by the events of World War I left the helicopter several leagues behind. The most common method of combating torque – the Newtonian equal and opposite reaction to the spinning rotor that tends to force the fuselage to turn in the opposite direction – was still to offset it by another rotor, spinning in the opposite direction (contra-rotating) either on the same axis (co-axial) or another. The weight penalties of such complex configurations were frequently prohibitive. The mysteries of cyclic pitch for directional control had been addressed by Ellehammer, but collective pitch was still rare, increased engine revolutions alone being relied upon to lift the machine from the ground. Forward speed, should horizontal flight be attained, was frequently minimal, with streamlining thus far unknown.

While many rotary-wing experiments floundered on the problems of the undesirable side-effects of a powered rotor, a young Spaniard, Don Juan de la Cierva, was instrumental in discovering a short cut to rotor-borne flight. His solution – not to power the rotor at all! His interest had stemmed from first rebuilding and then designing fixed-wing aircraft, an occupation that had led to the construction of a large three-engined bomber-transport in 1917. When it was lost in a steep turn at low altitude, Cierva pondered the possibility of designing an aircraft with a moving wing, mounted above the fuselage, which might render the machine stall-proof. Fixed-wing aircraft were unable to fly below a certain speed for fear of losing lift; if he could prove his concept worked, the result could be the safest form of air transport yet.

Cierva soon discarded the flapping-wing ornithopter concept that had consistently proved unworkable in past centuries, opting instead for a large propeller-like structure mounted above the fuselage's center of gravity on a pylon. Three years of research and development later, he flew his first rotary-wing machine, the C-4, at Madrid on 9 January 1923, calling it an 'autogiro'. In very many respects it resembled a streamlined conventional aircraft, with a pusher-configuration propeller providing forward propulsion and conventional tail surfaces. Any problems of lift dissymmetry had been solved by adopting a crude passive cyclic pitch control, permitting the rotor blades to flap up (reducing lift) and down (increasing

lift) on hinges to equalize lift on either side of the fuselage as the airflow caused by the machine's forward motion kept the rotor blades 'windmilling'.

Cierva continued his researches through the twenties, licensing his concept to many fledgling aircraft manufacturers worldwide. Many emulated Cierva's previous experiences of rebuilding crashed aircraft by turning their attention to war-surplus airframes such as the Avro 504 basic trainer, and it was one of these 'recycled' machines, designated C8L, that made the first rotary-wing flight across the English Channel on 18 September 1928. Cierva himself was the pilot on this occasion, having finally learned to fly the previous year.

The first half of the following decade saw Cierva enhance the autogiro's take-off capability by introducing the jumpstart. Previous designs had required a take-off run (albeit short) to start the rotor turning. By connecting the engine to the rotor, it could be pre-rotated in fine pitch before being declutched. With drive then directed to the tractor propeller, the rotor's pitch was increased and something akin to a helicopter's vertical take-off was achieved. It was at this time, too, that the horizontal flying surfaces previously retained for control in the rolling plane were discarded in favour of direct control of the rotor disc effected by the pilot via a lever connecting hub to cockpit.

Cierva's death, ironically in a fixed-wing airliner accident at Croydon in 1936, signaled the end of inter-war autogiro development. Yet less than two decades of research had put the autogiro – and rotary-winged flight – firmly on the aviation map. His licenses had provided manufacturers from the United States to the USSR with their first introduction to rotary-wing design and production. And while the even faster development of the helicopter was to relegate the autogiro to sporting use only, the concept had proved a valuable 'halfway house' between fixed-wing aircraft and the helicopter.

Before delving yet deeper into the annals of rotorcraft history, it is worth considering the objectives toward which the previously mentioned pioneers were moving in so slow and unsure a fashion. The generation and variation of lift was an obvious first priority, and one which at first consideration might seem to be merely a matter of increasing engine revolutions. Not so: for apart from being an inefficient method of regulation, obviously limited by the power of the engine, the time lag between opening the throttle and attaining the desired revolutions would preclude flight in all but the most predictable of conditions. Directional control, too, posed problems; parallels with fixed-wing flight suggested control surfaces on the rotating blades. But how to operate them; where to site them; and what of the torque that exerted such a force on the fuselage of

Opposite top: J C Ellehammer's pioneering design lifted from the ground but could not sustain flight.

Opposite below: An Fw 261 is moved out onto the runway. Like many designs of the period it was clearly derived from a fixed-wing type, the Fw 44 Stieglitz.

Below: A typical early Cierva autogiro, combining the fuselage and engine of a fixed-wing aircraft with a rotor and 'paddle' ailerons mounted where the lower wing would have been.

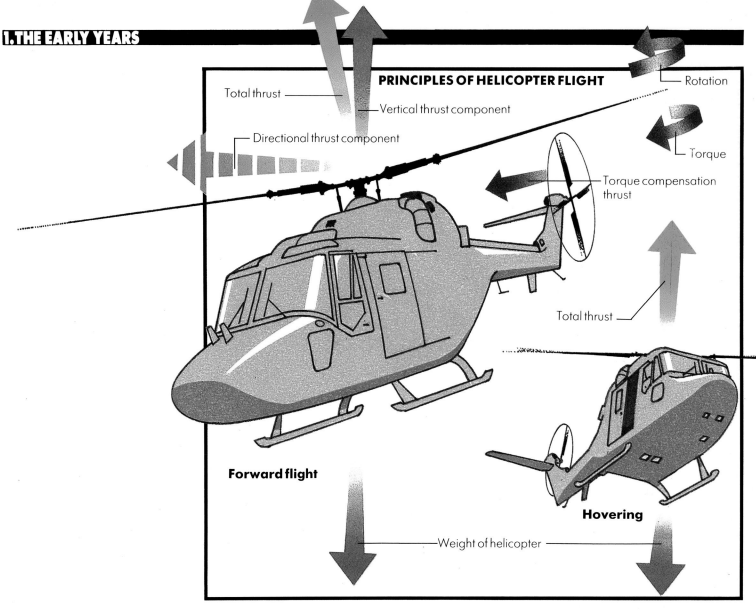

PRINCIPLES OF HELICOPTER FLIGHT

Total thrust

Vertical thrust component

Directional thrust component

Rotation

Torque

Torque compensation thrust

Total thrust

Forward flight

Hovering

Weight of helicopter

single-rotor helicopters? For the answers to these questions, let us examine now the single main rotor helicopter of the modern era.

The helicopter's main rotor generates lift in the same way as a conventional airscrew on a fixed-wing aircraft. Rather than merely increasing the speed of rotation to produce more lift, the pitch of the blades is altered, causing them to pivot together (collectively) to bite into the air more effectively and produce more lift. As soon as the lift obtained is greater than the weight of the helicopter, it will rise. As the blades' angle of attack is increased they not only provide more lift but also provide greater resistance to the airflow, as they rotate, than in the nearly flat fine pitch position, where they lie at only two or three degrees to the horizontal. In consequence, extra power is called for to maintain the speed of revolution, and this is supplied either by a mechanical linkage or, with more sophisticated turbine-powered helicopters, by the fuel control system. The collective pitch lever is to be found to the left of the pilot's seat.

Collective pitch variation, then, is responsible for controling vertical lift, in which the rotor spins horizontally on its axis. Directional control is achieved by tilting the

rotor disc to give a horizontal (forward or, sometimes, sideways) component to the lift being created. The resultant force will be a combination of the vertical and horizontal components which, if the vertical lift remains equal to the weight of the helicopter, will propel it 'straight and level' in the desired direction. This tilting of the rotor disc is achieved by means of the cyclic pitch control, usually situated – like a conventional aircraft's control column – between the pilot's knees.

Cyclic pitch also has the function of equalizing lift within the rotor disc during horizontal flight – for, while the lift provided by each blade remains constant in purely vertical flight, the blades' speed will vary when the helicopter is in forward motion. When a blade advances, its airspeed relative to the airflow increases – and so, therefore, does its lift. The reverse is true for the retreating blade, in other words the one which has passed the directional (fore-aft) axis and is retreating in an arc from nose to tail. The blades are permitted to 'flap' up and down, and will tend to flap up (due to increased lift) when advancing and down (due to diminished lift) when retreating. But the upward-flapping blade will lose lift since its angle of attack relative to the airflow will be

TYPICAL ROTOR HEAD

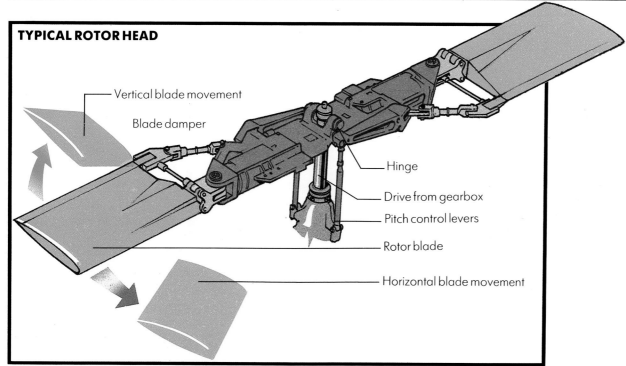

Vertical blade movement

Blade damper

Hinge

Drive from gearbox

Pitch control levers

Rotor blade

Horizontal blade movement

diminished, while the downward-flapping blade will find its angle of attack – and therefore its lift – increasing. The end result is that the gains and losses in lift cancel each other out, yet the movements of the blades up and down continue, causing the disc to tilt backwards. The pilot corrects this tendency to climb by pushing his cyclic pitch control forward, altering the pitch of the individual blades to give the advancing blade an even more reduced pitch angle and the retreating blade a yet greater pitch angle: this restores longitudinal stability by tilting the disc forward once more.

The necessity for both collective and cyclic pitch controls results in the helicopter's Achilles heel – the rotor head. Since the shaft connecting the rotor to the engine cannot physically be moved forwards, backwards or sideways, rotating as it does at many revolutions per second, directional (cyclic pitch) control is most commonly accomplished by a two-piece 'swash plate'. This consists of two similarly-sized circular plates connected by a bearing. The upper tilts and rotates with the rotor blades, to which it is attached by rods. The lower – to which the control transmission is linked – merely tilts. Cyclic pitch changes required to obtain changes in direction may be obtained by tilting the lower swash plate, which then imparts the same change to the angle of the upper component. This movement is transmitted by the push-pull rods and results in cyclic pitch changes as the blades move around the rotor disc. Collective pitch changes are usually effected by moving both portions of the swash plate up or down the rotor shaft, thereby affecting all blades equally.

The inter-relation of the helicopter's controls is complex indeed. A change from hovering to forward horizontal flight, for

example, would necessitate an immediate increase in collective pitch, since some of the vertical component of the lift will have been translated into horizontal propulsion. This increase in collective pitch may be accompanied by an overall increase in power, which will in its turn increase the torque developed by the main rotor. The tail rotor, whose function it is to offset this torque, will therefore require an increase in collective pitch (simply controled by orthodox rudder pedals) to keep the helicopter on a constant heading.

The helicopter, then, can be defined as having a powered main rotor or rotors, creating a downward flow of air through which the pilot exercises directional control in all planes of flight. Autogiros, as discussed, rely on a free-spinning rotor (powered by air flowing up through it) for their vertical lift, all motive power being supplied by a horizontally-opposed engine. Three other terms complete the rotary wing vocabulary. A compound helicopter is one whose fixed wing and/or propellers offload the powered rotor in flight, providing additional lift. A convertiplane can convert during flight from rotor-derived lift to fixed wings and vice versa. Finally, a vertoplane's propellers and rotors are one and the same, the power plants tilting to function in both the vertical and horizontal planes. The last two categories, to a certain extent, overlap with the fixed wing realm and are only included in this book where they are of particular interest.

Hardly surprisingly, the complexities of design and mechanics evident in today's rotorcraft were rarely to be found in fully developed form in machines designed prior to World War II. Indeed, compared with Cierva's inspired experiments, the true helicopter was really proceeding at a snail's pace. One of the most persistent of those who continued its development was Raoul Pescara, an Argentine citizen domiciled in Europe. His first machine, flown in Spain in 1920, was not successful, but his No. 3 helicopter established a distance record of 736 meters (805 yards) in France four years later. Though his machine was clumsy in appearance, with its contra-rotating, coaxial four-bladed biplane rotors, it was significant in that it used both cyclic *and* collective pitch for its means of control. Furthermore, Pescara recognized the importance of permitting auto-rotation, the ability of the rotor to be declutched to 'windmill' in the same way as an autogiro rotor, to bring the craft safely down to earth in the case of engine failure. Sadly, however, his experiments were not as successful as he would have wished, and he retired in 1925.

The possibilities of the helicopter as a battlefield observation platform, supplementing the tethered balloons to be seen in profusion along the Front, had been noted during World War I when a moored rotorcraft powered by an electric motor was proposed by von Karman and Petrosczy of Germany. Several years later, the US Army showed interest in the design of G. du Bothezat, a Russian émigré, whose four-rotor machine underwent extensive evaluation. In the UK, meanwhile, the Air Ministry offered a prize of £50,000 for a viable helicopter. This was nearly won by Louis Brennan, an Irishman whose design for a single-rotor helicopter with propellers at the blade tips was built at the Royal Aircraft Establishment. Among the advantages of this concept was the complete absence of torque, the engine being suspended above the fuselage in a swiveling bearing, while blade warping for cyclic pitch control was provided by compressed-air-powered tabs. Its destruction in a crash in 1925, combined with the rapid rise of the autogiro, led to a lull in helicopter development in Britain and the prize went unclaimed.

Brennan's machine had been unusual in possessing only one main rotor – but its unusual configuration enabled the problem of torque to be ignored. This was not the case with most single-rotor helicopters, however, and the tail rotor concept proposed by Yuriev had been apparent in the 1924 design of Dutchman von Baumhauer. Though he showed wisdom in adopting the idea, he made the mistake of powering it by its own engine and incurring a prohibitive weight penalty, but the overall configuration nevertheless closely resembled the majority of helicopters of today.

Cierva's influence spilled over from the autogiro to the helicopter field, assisted by the large number of countries building his designs under license. In Italy, for example, d'Ascanio borrowed the flapping hinge concept (enabling the advancing blade to flap up and the retreating blade flap down) for his

own helicopter of 1930 and set the first internationally recognized helicopter records for altitude, distance and endurance. These were to stand for fully five years until broken by the Breguet-Dorand Gyroplan Laboratoire, the first Breguet rotary-wing design since the historic Breguet-Richet No. 1 of 1907. Though its initial speed record of fully 27 mph from a 350 hp Hispano-Suiza engine was hardly impressive, the type's good control characteristics helped it establish further records (a speed of 67 mph in December 1935 and endurance of 62 minutes eleven months later) and made his co-axial, metal-bladed helicopter a ground-breaker.

The appearance of the Focke Fw 61 in 1936 however, was to change the face of rotary wing flight. Henrich Focke had left Focke Wulf to found the Focke Achgelis concern, having gained invaluable experience in the license production of Cierva C19

Above: This electric-powered rotorcraft was evaluated as an observation platform during WW1. Designed by von Karman and Petrosczy of Germany, it was not singularly successful.

Left: Louis Brennan's design was one of the most promising of European rotorcraft between the wars. Its destruction in a crash in 1925 dealt a blow to helicopter development in Britain.

Left: Breguet's Gyroplan Laboratoire of 1935 set several speed and endurance records.

Right: B N Yuriev was an early Soviet rotorcraft pioneer whose espousal of the tail rotor concept proved far-sighted indeed.

Below: Von Baumhauer's 1924 design adopted Yuriev's suggestions, though the weight of an extra engine to drive the tail rotor imposed too great a weight penalty to permit flight.

and C30 autogiros. Like Cierva's early machines, Focke's first attempt used the fuselage of a surplus biplane trainer, in this case the Fw 44 Stieglitz. Outrigger pylons carried two fully articulated counter-rotating rotors driven by the 160 hp Siemens radial engine in the nose. First flown on 26 June 1936, the Fw 61 used both cyclic and collective pitch control, with differential-collective being used to play one rotor against the other and provide directional control, as with the Gyroplan Laboratoire. Variation in vertical lift, however, still relied on increasing rotor revolutions and control in this plane of flight was thus far from immediate.

The Fw 61 served notice of intent with a record speed of 76 mph in 1937, and in February of the following year demonstrated its controlability by being flown within Berlin's Deutschland Halle sports stadium by noted test pilot Hanna Reitsch. Germany's aviation industry was at this stage gearing up for war, and a military version, the Fa 223 Drache was soon put into production – the first helicopter ever to attain such status. Allied action limited its run to some 20 complete machines, and it was one of these that reached a record height of 23,294 ft in 1940. A postscript to the Drache's short history was written when a captured example became the first pure helicopter to cross the English Channel in 1945 when returning to the UK for post-war evaluation.

Focke was not the only rotorcraft manufacturer to supply the Reich. Anton Flettner's Fl 282 Kolibri was used by the German Navy for shipboard reconnaissance duties in the later war years. Its subsequent interest lay in the fact that changes in the pitch of the blades of the intermeshing twin rotors automatically controled engine revolutions, while engine failure resulted in a switch to autorotation (minimum) pitch – both astonishingly advanced features for the time.

Yet despite Germany's evident leaps ahead in rotorcraft technology, her lead was not to remain unchallenged. Igor Sikorsky, whose failures in 1909 and 1910 had led him to turn his attention to the design of fixed-wing aircraft (and thereby become one of the USSR's foremost manufacturers), had fled Russia during the revolution. From his new base in the US, he had continued designing and building fixed-wing landplanes, amphibians and, most famously, flying boats. Noting the advances being made in Europe, he turned his attentions once more to the rotary-wing sphere: the result was the VS-300, first flown (tethered) by its designer on 14 September 1939. Its significance was twofold – it was the first helicopter with a tail rotor to remain airborne for any appreciable period, and secondly it became the first in a long and distinguished line of Sikorsky rotorcraft.

The VS-300 was to be modified considerably during its four-year period of develop-

Far left: The Focke Achgelis Fa 223 Drache was the world's first helicopter to achieve production status.

Left: A captured example of the Flettner Fl 282 Kolibri reconnaissance helicopter. Note the type's intermeshing rotors.

Below: A Focke Achgelis unpowered autogiro is tried out by its American captors. Such machines were designed to provide reconnaissance platforms in wartime for naval surface vessels or submarines.

Right: Igor Sikorsky at the controls of the VS-300 as it makes its first (tethered) flight on 14 September 1934.

Below: The VS-300 at a later stage of development with streamlined fuselage fairing and floats.

Far right: Developed from the VS-300, the Sikorsky R-4 was the first helicopter to serve with the US Armed Forces.

ment. A three-rotor tail array, adopted to supplant cyclic pitch for directional control after an early crash, was soon superseded by the single tail rotor now considered standard. With a tandem two-seat all-glazed cockpit, this was to become known as the R-4 in its production version. On 6 May 1941, the VS-300 eclipsed the Focke Wulf Fw 61's endurance record with a flight of just over 92 minutes, while the fitting of pontoons had led to the world's first helicopter take-off from water in the previous month.

By 1943, when the VS-300 was retired to the Henry Ford Museum at Dearborn, Michigan, its R-4 derivative was already in service with the US Army Air Force. And history continued to be made with rapidity: on 6 May 1943 a YR-4B evaluation example was landed on the deck of the USS *Bunker Hill*, thereby achieving the world's first helicopter deck landing. The type also saw action when it joined the ranks of the US 1st Air Commando operating behind enemy lines in the Far East, the rescue of four downed airmen in April 1944 being the first mission of its type recorded. The US Navy took 25 examples with the designation HNS-1, while the British Royal Air Force and Fleet Air Arm between them acquired 52, naming the type Hoverfly 1.

What made the R-4 so special? Its combination of simplicity of layout (the single main rotor and tail rotor remained a Sikorsky trademark thereafter), effective cyclic and variable pitch controls effected by means of a 'spider' device (a precursor of the swash plate system in which the control rods pulled and pushed from above, responding to movements of a central column mounted within the hollow rotor shaft), and the ability to take more powerful engines; a 180 hp unit was standard from 1943. Furthermore, its fabric-covered construction was relatively easily maintained in the field.

Sikorsky was quick to demonstrate what was to become one of the cardinal rules of helicopter development: never stop refining your product. The R-4's final appearance had been shaped by more than 18 rebuilds and was understandably somewhat less than aerodynamically perfect. Sikorsky therefore transferred its rotor and transmission system to a new, more streamlined fuselage, with rounded Plexiglass moldings replacing the R-4's angular panes of cockpit glazing. Mainwheels were brought inboard from their previous vulnerable outrigger stations, and a small nosewheel was added to cope with sudden changes of incidence on the ground. A semi-monocoque metal tailboom replaced the R-4's rudimentary fabric-covered framework while a 240 hp Franklin engine gave production models of the R-6, as this new machine was designated, an extra power boost.

The first R-6 flew on 15 October 1943, two months after a parallel Sikorsky project, the R-5. The latter's resemblance to the R-6 aft

Right: The Sikorsky S-51 in civilian markings.

Below: A British European Airways (now British Airways) S-51 takes off from the center of London on an early air mail flight.

Top: The S-51 served in Korea as the R-5 where it fulfilled the casualty evacuation role.

Inset above: Sikorsky's R-6 was developed from the R-4 in time to serve in the closing years of World War II.

of the rotor was considerable, yet its extensively glazed cabin provided optimum visibility for two crew members, seated in tandem to provide a smaller fuselage cross-section. Two casualty litters could be carried, one on either side of the fuselage. It was the civil derivative of this, known as the S-51 in the company's own designation scheme, that was to help put the helicopter on the peacetime map.

As peace loomed, the future of the helicopter seemed considerably brighter than at any stage in its history, ironically due to its newly perceived value as a military tool. Indeed, this link between the helicopter and the armed forces was to prove crucial in supplying the necessary resources for the expensive and complex research which still remained. And, in many cases, civil spinoffs from military projects would prove a great success in their own field. The previously mentioned S-51 was a prime example of this. First flown in February 1946, it had grown from the original tandem-seat R-5 to become a genuine four-seater. Its service use helped

obtain civil certification as early as March, and deliveries commenced five months later. The S-51 inaugurated the world's first scheduled helicopter mail service with Los Angeles Airways in October 1947, repeating the feat in the UK in the following year with British European Airways. Westland built 165 examples in Britain as the Dragonfly, thus beginning a profitable association with Sikorsky that was to survive into the eighties. Meanwhile, examples of the improved four-seat S-51 found their way to the US Forces, where they served alongside the R-5As already in harness and performed casualty evacuation duties under fire in Korea with the USAF's Third Air Rescue Squadron and US Navy Helicopter Unit 1.

The helicopter had emerged from its chrysalis after many long and frustrating years of development. Thanks to Igor Sikorsky, it had spread its rotary wings for all to see. But in a world of peacetime austerity, it was soon clear that the helicopter would have to prove itself more than just an expensive plaything.

2 DEVELOPMENTS IN THE FIFTIES

Although Igor Sikorsky's wartime activities put him out in front in terms of rotorcraft development, his was not the first helicopter to achieve a commercial type approval certificate. This singular honor was conferred upon the Bell 47, a product of a company already known for the Cobra series of piston-engined fighters and the manufacture of America's first jet, the P-59A Airacomet. Larry Bell had flown his first experimental helicopter, the Model 30, in 1943 but, with pressure of vital wartime work, development was put on the back burner. Nevertheless the historic Bell 47 made its maiden flight days before the end of 1945. Its simplicity of construction and appearance marked it down as one of the classic designs: a Plexiglass bubble cockpit afforded its three occupants outstanding all-round visibility, while a steel tube open girder-style tail boom made for easy maintenance.

The Bell 47 was powered in early production versions by a 178 hp Franklin piston engine, giving it a maximum speed of some 92 mph. It pioneered a stabilizing system unique to Bell and developed by Arthur Young, whose work with models had originally convinced Larry Bell of the feasibility of a full-size helicopter in 1941. It took the form of a bar with weights at each tip, mounted at 90 degrees to the two rotor blades. This provided a stabilizing force that tended to maintain the rotor's horizontal position irrespective of the angle of the mast, the rotor being mounted on universal joints to permit such movement.

Once issued with its commercial licence and type certificate a matter of months after its first flight, the Bell 47 rolled off the production line in some considerable quantity. Its civil applications were soon to become apparent; by the end of 1951, for example, 100 were estimated to be in use as agricultural crop-sprayers, being fitted with wide, forward-swept spray booms for the purpose. But inevitably it was the US armed forces, which had endorsed Bell's first helicopter as the XR-12 in the war years, whose interest was to boost production by the greatest amount. The outbreak of war in Korea was to see the Bell 47, in its guise as the H-13D (Army) and HTL-4 (Marine Corps), operate in the liaison, transport and cable-laying roles before being pressed into service for casualty evacuation. The wheeled landing gear of early examples had given way to the now-familiar skids, upon which litters would be lashed; up to seven persons were known to have been carried on exceptional missions. In 1951 alone, over 8500 casualties were plucked from the front line by Bell helicopters, to be transported to mobile hospitals miles to the rear of the fighting.

The Model 47 meanwhile continued to flourish in the civil sphere, where its unusually wide cabin visibility made it a favored mount of law enforcement agencies, forestry commissions, geological and geophysical surveyors, powerline inspectors and firefighters. The first major change in appearance occurred with the introduction of the 47J Ranger, a four-seat development in which the pilot sat in front of his three passengers in a larger cockpit. The tail

Previous page: An early-production Westland Whirlwind operated on floats by British European Airways.

Right: Pannier-equipped Bell 47 helicopters evacuated the wounded in Korea for the US Army, in whose service they were designated H-13.

Above: In the civil sphere, the Bell 47 found numerous applications. The good visibility from its Plexiglass bubble cockpit suiting it to observation, police and related roles. A Bell 47G-5 is illustrated.

boom was also enclosed at this time. Two luxuriously-equipped Rangers were supplied for the personal use of President Eisenhower, while the US Navy adopted the type as their standard training and utility helicopter, the HTL-7/HUL-1.

Production of ever-improved versions of the Bell 47 continued until 1962. When Bell's own line shut, Kawasaki (Japan), Westland (Britain) and Agusta (Italy) were still to add their license-produced machines to the total deliveries, which finally numbered some 6000 worldwide. An attempt to use the type's rotor mechanism for a larger project, the ten-seat Model 48 (USAF designation YH-12) was less successful, a small pre-production batch only being built. Ironically the Bell Helicopter Corporation was to produce the world's most widely used utility helicopter (the UH-1) a mere decade later, but this first attempt proved something of a false start.

Similar concepts to those of the Bell 47 had been employed in the Hughes Model 269 and the Hiller Model 360; the latter, indeed, shared the Bell 47's choice of power plant. Stanley Hiller Jr. had demonstrated his co-axial XH-44 in August 1944, developing it two years later to become the UH-4 Commuter. The Model 360, later to become more readily known by the designation UH-12, was of more conventional appearance with a main and tail rotor but was unusual in another respect. Directional control was maintained by means of an overhead 'stick' operating a control rotor projecting at right angles to the two main rotor blades with mini movable flying surfaces or 'paddles' at

each end. When operated by the pilot, the pitch changes of this control rotor governed the behavior of the blades with which it was interposed by means of tilting the rotor head in a system known as Rotor-Matic. A more conventional control column and collective pitch lever were later introduced, and this undoubtedly helped accelerate the type's adoption by the US armed forces as a training and observation type. The Canadian Army also made use of the type, while the British Royal Navy employed 21 of the OH-23G variant as a basic trainer.

The Hughes 269 also found favor as a training machine, its minimum structure permitting little more than its two occupants to be squeezed in. Adopted by the US Army in 1964 as the TH-55A Osage, some 792 examples were purchased in all. The Vietnam War had placed extra demands on the helicopter pilot-training machinery, and the vast majority of US Army 'chopper' pilots to fly in the Southeast Asia theater had been introduced to rotary-wing flight by the TH-55A. A larger derivative of the Model 269, the Hughes Model 300, had been launched in 1957. Production was transferred to Schweizer Aircraft in 1983, by which time over 2750 Hughes-built examples had been ordered for training, police and agricultural work.

Igor Sikorsky's concern had not rested on its laurels since the R-5 (S-51) was granted its Certificate of Airworthiness in 1946. The next development to emerge from their Bridgeport, Connecticut, factory was the S-52. A smaller helicopter than its predeces-

Left: Final development of the Bell 47 was the enclosed-boom Model 47J Ranger.

Right: The diminutive Hughes 300, seen here in civilian markings, was most widely used as a military trainer by the US Army as the TH-55 Osage.

Below: The simplicity of the Hiller UH-12 ensured a ready market in the agricultural field. The UH-12E here is fitted with spray booms and chemical tanks amidships.

Top: The installation of a Gnome turbine engine gave the Whirlwind a new lease of life; a Royal Navy Mark 9 is pictured.

Above: Soviet rotorcraft pioneer Mikhail Mil.

Opposite above: US Marine Sikorsky H-19s airlift ammunition to a rocket battery in Korea.

Opposite: Developed from the Sikorsky S-55/H-19 series, Westland's Whirlwind made its name as an air-sea rescue helicopter in Royal Air Force service.

sor, which it replaced in US Marine Corps service, it was nevertheless a genuine three/occasional four seater. It was first flown in 1947 and in the following year captured three world records for speed and height, but such innovations as all-metal rotor blades were not to weigh in its favor: a smaller, more compact S-51 was clearly not the number one priority at this stage. What was needed was a helicopter with real troop-carrying capacity. And once more Sikorsky had the answer.

The S-55 first flew on 7 November 1949 and was a very significant helicopter indeed. Adopting the rotor mechanism and drives of the S-52, it was powered by a 600 hp Pratt & Whitney Wasp radial mounted not aft but in the nose, a sloping drive shaft communicating with the gear box. A large passenger cabin seating up to ten troops was achieved by siting the cockpit on top, looking out over the sloping engine hood. The configuration improved visibility, engine accessibility (via two clam-shell nose doors) and cabin size at a stroke, while a power-operated hoist combined with a sliding door to facilitate winching casualties aboard while hovering in mid-air. All this added up to a considerable advance on the S-51, and the US armed forces were not slow to show their appreciation; over half of the production run of 1828 was snapped up by the US Air Force, Army, Navy and Marine Corps. The H-19, as it was

designated, followed the R-5 into Korea in March 1951 on the strength of the USAF's Air Rescue Squadrons and rapidly proved its worth. More than 20 air forces worldwide were to operate the S-55, while over 550 were built under license in Japan, France and Britain.

British license manufacture was undertaken by Westland Aircraft at Yeovil in Somerset where 485 examples, named Westland Whirlwind, were produced for the Royal Air Force, Navy and others. Many improvements were made during the course of the production run, including the replacement of the original Wright or Pratt & Whitney engine by first a 750 hp Alvis Leonides piston and then a Bristol Siddeley Gnome turbine. The yellow-painted Whirlwinds of RAF Coastal Command were to become a legend around Britain's coast saving thousands of lives in air-sea rescues.

The Whirlwind also wrote itself a page of rotorcraft history when it took part in the Anglo-French assault at Suez in 1956, this being the first occasion on which the British armed forces employed helicopters operationally. Soldiers from 45 Royal Marine Commando were flown ashore on 6 November from the carriers HMS *Ocean* and *Theseus* to back up a conventional seaborne assault, which had itself been preceded by a parachute landing the day before. Since little resistance was met in terms of ground fire, the helicopter landing was achieved with total success.

The focus of attention in the rotorcraft world had fallen fairly and squarely on the United States, and Sikorsky in particular, in those postwar years. Yet Sikorsky's flight to the West had by no means left the Soviet Union devoid of rotary wing visionaries. It took one of these who remained, Mikhail Mil, whose second major design, the Mi-4, appeared in 1953 to remind the Western allies of that fact.

Mikhail Mil had grown up with an engineering background, his father having been a mining engineer. His studies took him to the newly formed Novocherkassk Aviation Institute where, in 1929, he had assisted in the building of the KaSkr-1 autogiro. Graduating two years later, he continued in the rotary wing area under N. I. Kamov at the Central Aero and Hydrodynamics Institute (TsAGI), helping to design the A-12 and A-15 autogiros before the start of World War II.

The Mi-4 bore an uncanny resemblance to Sikorsky's S-55 with the two crew members seated side by side atop a large cabin. It was, however, significantly larger, with a 14-passenger capacity, and its 1700 hp Shvetsov ASh-82V piston engine – considerably more powerful than the 800 hp Wright of production S-55s – took it to a number of international records in 1956. These included a height record of 19,843 ft (6048 m) and a speed record of 116 mph (186 km/h) over a 500 km course.

The Mi-4's progress to flight-test status in only seven months had been due to Stalin's personal insistence that the Soviet Union should be able to rival the US capabilities shown by their recent operations in Korea. And this faith proved completely justified; like the Sikorsky S-58, to which it was perhaps more directly comparable, the Mi-4 (NATO code-name Hound) became a true maid of all work. It became an interim gunship with the addition of machine guns and rocket pods, was pressed into anti-submarine service prior to the advent of the purpose-built Mi-14 Haze and was later seen with electronic countermeasures aerials. The type was also produced in China as the Whirlwind-25.

It is possible that Mil might have been influenced by Sikorsky's design given the four-year gap between the S-55 and Mi-4. Yet he had already shown his intentions with the Mi-1, flown in 1948 and similar in both size and configuration to the Sikorsky S-51. It was the first Russian helicopter to be produced in quantity, being selected ahead of the single-rotor Yak-100 and twin-rotor Bratukhin designs, and served in both civil and military roles for very many years. Improvements made during the type's long production run, first in the USSR and then in Poland, confirmed that Mil fully intended to catch up with the progress of his Western counterparts.

Right: The helicopter has been of immense value in helping the Soviet Union open up its more inhospitable regions — and none more so than the workhorse Mil Mi-4. It is seen here helping in the construction of the Baikal-Amur railway.

Inset far right: An export version of the Mi-4 in Finnish service.

Above: The Soviet Mil Mi-1 has enjoyed a long and successful career since first flown in 1948.

Top: Conceived by Saunders Roe, the Scout was manufactured in quantity by Westland for the British Army Air Corps.

Opposite: Re-engined with twin Bristol Siddeley Gnome turboshafts, the Sikorsky S-58 became the Westland Wessex. A Wessex of the Royal Navy's No 845 Squadron is pictured during operations in Borneo, 1964.

The helicopter's ability to land in areas inaccessible to fixed-wing aircraft led to many early experiments delivering mail. Chicago, Los Angeles and New York all staged such exercises, and the carriers in each city all went on to establish city center to airport passenger services in the wake of their air mail operations. Similar experiments were tried and discontinued in the west of England by the Post Office and British European Airways, but the concept's most lasting success was inevitably achieved in areas such as Scandinavia and Canada where adverse weather conditions made regular mail delivery otherwise impossible. In these cases, the helicopter's high running costs could be more readily justified.

The development of the turbine engine was to prove the single biggest factor in the history of rotorcraft since the internal combustion engine. Just as the turboprop had conferred the virtues of fuel economy and quietness of operation upon the airliner, so

the helicopter stood to benefit from the turbine's application. What was more, the reduced size and weight of the new units promised obvious advantages. Consider the case of the Sikorsky S-58, developed to meet a US Navy specification for an anti-submarine helicopter with a greater range and payload than that of the S-55. The prototype flew on 8 March 1954, and the type was the subject of orders from all US services. The S-58's 1525 hp Wright Cyclone radial was over twice the size of the S-55's power plant and offered a payload increase of some 70 percent.

Although the US Navy was confident enough to order the type before the prototype had even flown, performance failed to live up to expectation. Westland in the UK purchased a license in 1956 to manufacture the S-58 (as the Wessex) as a follow-on project to their production of the S-55 as the Whirlwind. The deal included a US Navy HSS-1 Seabat, as that service designated the type, and Westland re-engined this on arrival with an indigenous Napier Gazelle II shaft turbine. The installation resulted in the Wessex's distinctive 'drooping' nose profile, but – more importantly – expanded the type's performance envelope considerably.

The final stage in Westland's development was initiated in January 1962, when a Wessex HAS Mark 1 was flown with twin Bristol Siddeley Gnome shaft turbines. This extended its maximum range to 478 miles (as opposed to the S-58's original 247 miles), as well as providing the added safety factor of two engines. The Wessex was rightly acclaimed as the world's most capable anti-submarine and transport helicopter then developed. The US Navy had pioneered the hunter/killer tactic for ASW operations, pairing one S-58 (in 'hunter' configuration with dipping sonar lowered into the water while hovering) with a torpedo-equipped 'killer'. The Wessex, with its improved per-

ROYAL NAVY XS566 DANGER

501

Left: The Westland Wasp shipboard helicopter emerged from the same P.531 private venture as the army Scout, an uprated Nimbus turboshaft, folding tail and castoring-wheel undercarriage being distinguishing features.

Right: A Wasp is made fast aboard ship. Note 'pigeon-toes' undercarriage position, obviating unwanted movement.

formance, could combine the two roles. Used as a transport, the Wessex could carry up to 16 troops, seven stretchers or 4000 pounds of freight, and a simplified assault transport version was developed for Royal Navy Commando duties as the HU Mark 5.

Westland had been building fixed-wing types for the Royal Air Force since 1916. Their first venture into the helicopter field had been with license production of the Sikorsky S-51, an agreement to that effect having been signed in 1947. A developed version, using a Whirlwind-type rotor head and a new forward fuselage, named Widgeon, had been designed, but found few customers. Nevertheless, this tactic of improving on the original Sikorsky design was the starting point of several Westland successes.

The Whirlwind and Wessex, then, were far from Westland's only ventures into the rotary-wing field, although indigenous designs had initially been comparatively modest in size. The Scout and Wasp, light liaison and anti-submarine helicopters for the Army and Navy respectively, were both variants of the private venture Saunders Roe P531 first flown on 20 July 1958. (Saunders Roe, together with Bristol's rotorcraft division, were incorporated into Westland by Government decree in 1960.) The Wasp differed from the Scout in having a more powerful 710 shp (685 shp) Bristol Siddeley Nimbus turboshaft, folding tail for shipboard storage and four-wheel castoring undercarriage. Both types joined the ranks of their respective UK services in 1963 and were to become the subject of modest export orders from Bahrain, Jordan, Uganda and Australia (Scout) and Brazil, Netherlands, New Zealand and South Africa (Wasp). In Army Air Corps service, the Scout followed the rather less successful Saunders Roe Skeeter, a two-seat light observation helicopter from the same stable. Although it had claimed the distinction of being the service's first rotorcraft, lack of power had seen it replaced not long after its introduction to service in 1957.

Rivaling Westland as Europe's leading rotorcraft manufacturer was France's Sud Aviation, the company formed by the merger of Sud-Est and Sud-Ouest in 1957. Their first excursion into the rotorcraft field (as Sud Est) was under the auspices of Professor Heinrich Focke soon after World War II when a six-seat development of the Focke Fa 223, designated SE.3000, was flown. Several experimental machines followed, but found little success until the advent of the Alouette.

Originally intended as an agricultural rotorcraft when first flown on 31 July 1951, the Alouette blossomed into a family of helicopters that represented a significant pillar in the postwar reconstruction of France's aircraft industry. The design owed much to the Bell 47 with its open-girder tail boom, and in its initial form, powered by a 200 hp Salmson 9NH radial engine, established an international helicopter flight

duration record of 13 hours 56 minutes. The SE.3120, as it was first designated, was then redesigned to accommodate a 360 shp Turboméca Artouste turboshaft, and it was in this form as the Alouette II that it was to make its mark. The new power plant conferred much improved performance at higher altitudes, a fact soon demonstrated by the establishment of a world height record for helicopters in June 1958 of 36,027 ft (10,984 m). By late 1960, over 600 Alouettes had been ordered by customers in 22 countries. The SA.313B was joined shortly afterwards on the production line by the SA.318C Alouette II Astazou, powered by the more economical Astazou engine and featuring a new centrifugal clutch. This helped boost the mark's popularity still further, and production of both marks had reached 1300 when the line was closed in 1975. Over 450 of these had found homes with the French armed forces.

Having cut their teeth on a simple yet

effective design, Aérospatiale followed the accepted policy of rotorcraft development to produce a big sister to the Alouette II. From all appearances, this bore the same relationship to its predecessor as the Bell 47J Ranger to the original Bell 47 (enclosed tail boom, larger cabin), but was in fact considerably bigger and more capable. The SE.3160 Alouette III first flew on 28 February 1959 and rapidly proved its abilities by such publicity stunts as landing on and taking off fully laden from Mont Blanc in the French Alps at an altitude of 15,780 ft (4810 m). Not surprisingly, many sales were to operators in such hot and/or high environments as Switzerland, India, Saudi Arabia and Zaire.

The Alouette III enjoyed two decades in production, its popularity boosted not only by improvements to the Astazou engine but the growing realization of its capabilities as a sturdy, adaptable two-seat light attack helicopter armed with guns, cannon and

Above: Sud Aviation followed the Alouette II with the larger and more capable III, seen here operating as an air ambulance in the United States.

Opposite above: The Saunders Roe Skeeter light observation helicopter was underpowered, and served only briefly with the British Army Air Corps.

Opposite: The Alouette II was one of European rotorcraft's major successes of the 1950s and 1960s. A powerful Lama model is pictured.

Right: Although it was not one of their more famous designs, Sikorsky's S-56 Mojave proved a useful troop-carrying workhouse for the US Armed Forces.

Below: Piasecki's HUP-1 Retriever was an ancestor of the world-famous Boeing Vertol twin rotor types.

Left: Known colloquially as 'Flying Bananas,' Piasecki's tandem-rotor designs were widely used in the 1950s. This H-21 Shawnee served with the West German army.

Above: A US Marine descends from a US Marine Corps Boeing Vertol CH-46D Sea Knight.

Opposite above: Boeing's commercial Chinook is one of the most impressive civil helicopters ever, and looks set to continue in production into the 1990s.

Opposite: Charles H Kaman experimented with a twin intermeshing rotor system on his K-225 in the late 1940s. The result was a successful range in the following decade.

air for the first time on 18 December 1953, it was progressively updated in US Army service and soldiered on until supplanted by the S-61R/H-3 in the late sixties.

The twin-rotor layout that had characterized nearly all the real or projected helicopters prior to Sikorsky's VS-300 had not entirely fallen into disuse with the discovery of the anti-torque tail rotor. The twin-rotor school of design divided itself into three streams: tandem rotors, intermeshing rotors and co-axial rotors. A main proponent of the twin-rotor theory had been Frank Piasecki, the first US pilot to gain a helicopter license. His first helicopter, the PV-2, flew on 11 April 1943 to become the second successful American helicopter (although it was to prove the only single-rotor design he ever built). Encouraged by this success, he turned his hand to a larger design with more obvious military applications. His answer to the problem of limited piston-engine power – to double not engines but rotors! Piasecki's 'banana-fuselage' H-21 Shawnee, with its capacity of 20 troops or 12 stretchers, was the first helicopter to boast a hydraulic hoist; it was ordered in quantity by the US Air Force (about 200) and Army (334). Delivered in the early fifties, many Army machines soldiered on to serve in the early days of Vietnam. The much smaller HUP-1 (later UH-25) Retriever was a favorite of the US Navy, which purchased 265 examples for carrier operation. Both types also attracted limited foreign orders.

The tandem-rotor concept was adopted enthusiastically by the Vertol Aircraft Corporation, formed under Piasecki's presidency in March 1956, as it sought to design a successful twin-engined transport helicopter. Turboshafts (General Electric T58s in production examples) were wisely selected as offering a better power to weight ratio than equivalent piston engines – a farsighted move for the time – and were installed above the fuselage at the rear to leave the passenger and freight area unencumbered. Entrance to a capacious hold that could accommodate up to 25 troops or 15 stretcher cases was effected via a folddown rear loading ramp.

The Vertol Model 107 first flew on 22 April 1958 and, after extensive development and demonstration, won a design competition for a US Marine Corps medium assault transport. As the CH-46 Sea Knight, it served the USMC for over two decades while the US Navy operated the type as the UH-46 in the VERTREP role, vertically replenishing the stores, personnel and ammunition of ships at sea. Civil and military examples were also built under license by Kawasaki.

The US Army's initial interest in the Model 107 was switched to a larger derivative, the Model 114 or CH-47 Chinook, designed to fulfill an exacting all-weather heavy-lift specification. In addition to being asked to carry a 2-ton load internally or 8

missiles. Most popular choice of anti-tank missile was the Aérospatiale AS.11, four of which could be carried on bolt-on launcher 'arms' simply attached to the fuselage. Many Third World countries pressed the type into service in the attack role, while India elected to develop a specialized derivative known as the HAL Chetak, following on in the eighties from 200 standard license-built machines. The Alouette III was also manufactured in Romania (130) and Switzerland (60).

Although it emerged as one of Sikorsky's less spectacular designs, the S-56 (or H-37 Mojave, as the US Army and Marine Corps styled it) was one of the first purpose-built assault transport helicopters to fly. Its clam-shell nose loading doors and ramp offered quick, easy loading of 36 equipped troops or equivalent freight. The Mojave enjoyed a long and useful life; taking to the

tons underslung, it was expected to seat 40 troops and airlift any component of the forthcoming Pershing missile system. The Chinook fulfilled all these requirements and more, going on to prove its worth in Vietnam where it recovered downed aircraft, airlifted refugees, acted as a flying casualty ward and transported troops and supplies. Indeed such was its value that the Royal Air Force ordered a number of Chinooks some two decades after first flight to serve as their chief heavy-lift helicopter into the next century. These immediately justified their purchase by serving with distinction in the Falklands War of 1982. Boeing, which had meanwhile taken over Vertol Helicopters in 1960, also developed a commercial Chinook for offshore oilfield support work. With 44-passenger capacity, Boeing 727 windows, glassfiber rotor blades and more powerful engines, this most capable Chinook yet seemed likely to keep the type in production to the end of the eighties and possibly beyond.

The Royal Air Force had possessed its own home-grown heavy lift helicopter in the Westland Belvedere, similar in configuration to the Chinook but plagued by development problems that were uniquely and sadly its own. Westland inherited the Belvedere, originally a navy project, from Bristol, whose chief contribution to British rotorcraft history had previously been the Model 171 Sycamore. Designed by émigré Austrian Raoul Hafner, it had been the first helicopter designed and built in Britain after World War II. The Type 173, from which

Right: The Bristol Sycamore was the first helicopter to be designed and built in Britain after World War II.

Opposite: The worlds most famous tandem-rotor, the Boeing Vertol CH-47 Chinook, in Vietnam with the US Army.

Below: The Belvedere utilized Sycamore components and, after a protracted development period, followed its single-rotor predecessor into RAF service.

the Belvedere derived, was intended to follow the five-seat communications helicopter into RAF service and, indeed, was very nearly a 'double Sycamore' in employing its engines and rotor components. But ground vibration – an unsympathetic vibration of undercarriage, fuselage and rotor – meant that it took eight months from its May 1951 rollout to achieve even a ten-minute flight.

The project never really recovered, even though the Belvedere finally entered RAF service in September 1961. Despite the type's prodigious lift capacity – aircraft, radio telescope dishes, small helicopters and missiles being underslung with equal ease – poor cabin access and restricted internal dimensions, both legacies of its original purpose, made it unsuitable for the transport of freight and troops. It was withdrawn from service after less than a decade, leaving the RAF without a heavy lift helicopter until the advent of the Chinook.

Another tandem rotor machine to deserve passing mention was Yakovlev's Yak-24, very much a contemporary of the Bristol project and one which, too, suffered innumerable development problems; vibration of the main rotors led to a delay in production of five months. Nevertheless the 24-seater Yak-24 was the world's largest helicopter when first flown, with a fuselage length of 70 ft, rotor diameter of 69 ft and a gross weight of 35,275 pounds. Range, however, was poor at 125 miles and – perhaps significantly – it was Yakovlev's last stab at the rotary-wing market.

The trademark of Charles H. Kaman's helicopter designs was the interesting twin-blade system pioneered during the war years by Flettner in Germany. A former employee of Sikorsky, Kaman left to form his own company in 1946 and immediately put some unusual ideas into practice. The first was two twin two-bladed rotors, mounted side by side on outward-canted masts and intermeshing not far from the hub. The second was a system of control known as servo tabs, small flaps that could be trimmed from the cockpit to move the blades.

His first helicopters pioneered these concepts in the late Forties, and were leased out by the company as crop dusters to prove their reliability. Examples of the K-225 were evaluated by the US Coast Guard and Navy in 1949, and the result was a major contract. The HTK-1 training helicopter and the HOK-1 observation helicopter shared both the intermeshing rotor configuration and Pratt & Whitney R-1340 piston power plant, serving with the Navy and Marine Corps respectively. Their unusual rotor arrangement was not the only distinguishing feature of these diminutive helicopters: twin booms extended from the boxy fuselage to support the tailplane which, thanks to the twin counter-rotating main rotors, needed no compensatory tail rotor.

Right: The heavy lift Yak-24 was the Yakovlev design bureau's only successful rotorcraft.

Below: Nikolai Kamov and students of the Moscow Aviation Institute.

Bottom: One of Kamov's successful creations, the Ka-18 four-seat helicopter. Note his trademark contra-rotating rotors on a common shaft.

A utility development of the HOK-1, the HUK, was entered in a US Air Force competition for a liaison helicopter, and the result was the H-43 Huskie. After production of an initial batch, the decision was made to utilize turbine power. By mounting the new Lycoming T53 engine above the cabin (exhausting through a long stack draped over the tailplane), usable cabin space was doubled at a stroke. While this was later to prove particularly useful in their sorties over the jungles of Vietnam, where the Huskie was successful in recovering many downed aircrew, it was as a crash rescue helicopter that the type excelled. Beating back the flames with its rotors to permit the safe rescue of survivors and carrying underslung firefighting equipment, the Huskie became a familiar sight at the bases of all US Air Force flying commands within the United States. Burma, Colombia and Iran also operated the type in small numbers.

Kaman had not severed its connections with the US Navy despite the Huskie finding favor with the Air Force, and when a replacement for the HUK-1 was sought Kaman was among the contenders. The winning design, the HU-2 Seasprite, broke with company tradition in being of 'conventional' main rotor/tail rotor configuration. Its retractable landing gear and watertight hull meant that operations could be mounted from land, ship or water, while the type's allotted tasks included carrier and replenishment work, reconnaissance, casualty evacuation and tactical air control. A surprisingly large load of 11 persons could be carried, but power was soon found to be no more than adequate and was doubled by the addition of

an extra 1250 shp General Electric T58 turboshaft; the two units being podded on either side of the rotor pylon. With the Seasprite having meanwhile been redesignated UH-2, the single engined A- and B- suffix variants were up-rated to twin standard alongside the new-build UH-2C.

The Seasprite was to be worked hard in Vietnam, where it was flown in HH-2C gunship configuration with armor plate and chin and waist-mounted pairs of 7.62 mm miniguns. The missions it was called upon to fly were typified by the flight of Lieutenant Clyde E. Lassen of US Navy Squadron HC-7, whose rescue of two downed airmen from a heavily defended stretch of North Vietnam coastline on 19 June 1968 won him the Medal of Honor.

The Seasprite's origins in the fifties did not prevent the US Navy converting examples of the HH-2D to fill the gap before the selection of a LAMPS (light airborne multi-purpose system) helicopter for the eighties. The system attempted to combine two important functions in ensuring the safety of US Navy surface vessels: anti-submarine warfare (ASW) and anti-ship surveillance and targeting (ASST). Its 'light-weight' prefix indicated operation from small vessels of the frigate, destroyer and cruiser classes, with ship-to-helicopter communications of paramount importance. Up-rating the Seasprite to SH-2F standard to carry out these tasks involved the fitting of search radar in a nose radome, a towed magnetic anomaly detector 'bird' and homing torpedoes to reinforce the defense of

Left: Kaman's Seasprite has enjoyed two decades of service with the US Navy. The SH-2F version pictured fulfilled that service's demanding LAMPS specification.

Below: The H-43 Huskie firefighter was Kaman's most famous design, an example being based at all US Air Force flying commands within the United States.

surface ships. Although the contest to find a purpose-built LAMPS system was eventually won by the Sikorsky SH-60B, the Seasprite showed how engine and avionics improvements could keep a well-designed helicopter in the front line for a couple of decades.

While Kaman eventually abandoned the intermeshing rotor concept, Soviet engineer Nikolai I. Kamov kept faith with the contra-rotating layout popular with so many pioneers of rotary-wing flight but flown successfully only by Breguet. First experiments had included single-seat ultra-light 'sky cycles', in the mold of the Focke Fa 223, being towed behind surface vessels to spot targets over the horizon. The Ka-8 and 10, as they were designated, aroused immediate interest from the AVMF, the Soviet naval air arm, and were followed by Kamov's first truly capable machine in the Ka-15. A side by side two-seater first flown in 1952, its co-axial configuration permitted a fuselage length of six inches less than 20 ft that immediately suited it to shipboard operation. The improved Ka-18 four-seater, which shared its predecessor's H-shape tail unit, power plant, four-wheel undercarriage and rotor system, followed it into limited shipboard service, as well as continuing to exploit the fields of crop spraying, air mail and ambulance duties the Ka-15 had already entered. In comparison with the Mil Mi-1, the Ka-18 was just over half the length and could offer over double its rival's range – both factors crucial to a shipboard helicopter, and ones which were to ensure Kamov a monopoly in the field in the sixties and beyond.

3 THE VIETNAM ERA

The US Army's requirement, announced in 1955, for a turbine-powered utility helicopter had inspired a design that was to prove one of the most adaptable and hard-working rotorcraft not only of the sixties but history itself: the Bell 204. The first of six prototypes flew on 22 October 1956, and by the end of 1958 all bar one were undergoing stringent service trials at three air force bases across the continent. Deliveries of the HU (later UH)-1A began in mid 1959, the type having become the US Army's first turbine powered aircraft of any kind, fixed or rotary wing, to be ordered by the service.

The type, named Iroquois but more commonly known as 'Huey' in deference to its original HU designation prefix, was to prove identifiably a Bell product by its retention of the stabilizing bar of the Bell 47, this time above (rather than below) the main rotor. In all other respects, however, it broke new ground for the manufacturer. Its 1100 shp Lycoming T53 turbine sat atop the cabin, exhausting to the rear, while its skid landing gear – this time without the Model 47's ground-handling wheels – was ideally suited to its utility role.

The Iroquis proved capable of performing any and every task allotted to it; casualty evacuation, gunship, dual-control instrument trainer, troop transport and SAR helicopter. Orders continued apace: the 850th US Army UH-1 was delivered in February 1964, and B, C, E, F, K, L and M-suffix variants gradually joined the ranks. The T53 turbine was eventually up-rated to 1400 shp, while the UH-1C had seen the introduction of a new wide-chord 'door hinge' rotor which increased both speed and maneuverability and was installed on all subsequent models. As if to underline its versatility, the UH-1E not only replaced the rotary-wing Kaman H-43 in US Marine Corps service, but also the fixed-wing Cessna O-1 Bird Dog – testimony to its all-round ability.

Bell had proposed an improved Model 204 as early as 1960, with relocation of the fuel cells permitting a pilot and 14 (as opposed to the previous 7) troops to be accommodated; it was assisted in this by a 2-foot fuselage stretch. These machines were designated Model 205 by Bell and UH-1D by the US Army; after successful flight trials (the first prototype flying on 16 August 1961), the sub-type was ordered in quantity.

The UH-1D was followed into production by the UH-1H, identical but for the more powerful (1400 shp) T53 turboshaft already applied to the UH-1C and subsequent variants. The UH-1D and H saw extensive service in Vietnam, evacuating casualties from forward areas and gaining an enviable reputation for reliability and relative invulnerability to small-arms fire. The Australian Brigade at Phuoc Tuy province claimed that a wounded man could be on the operating table within forty minutes of being hit, thanks to the UH-1. A further development increasing the type's safety margin was the adoption of a 1800 shp Pratt & Whitney Aircraft of Canada PT6T-3 power plant, this coupled turbine affording twin-engined reliability. The US Air Force, Navy and Marine Corps all followed the Canadian armed forces in ordering the UH-1N, which remained in production into the eighties.

The Model 212, as the UH-1N's civil counterpart was termed by its makers, became an extremely popular civil workhorse, its twin-engine configuration, avionics refit and stabilization controls assisting it to become the first helicopter to be FAA certificated for single-pilot IFR (instrument flight rules) operations with fixed floats. A four-blade rotor variant, the Model 412, was subsequently 're-converted' to military use by license builders Agusta of Italy, who marketed it in the eighties as the multi-role Griffon.

Perhaps the ultimate UH-1 spinoff, however, was the 18-seat Model 214ST Super Transport, a project originally developed as a military transport for Iran but redirected by Bell after the Islamic revolution. With twin 1625 shp General Electric CT7 turboshafts, it offered a high-density 18-passenger (plus two crew) interior and represented a major step forward from the 212 both in appearance and performance. Deliveries commenced in 1982, and there was every sign that the Super Transport would keep the production lines of the Model 204 and derivatives rolling through the 30 year mark.

Vietnam had proved the first conflict in which the helicopter had played a dominant – if not decisive – role. The movement of troops from barracks to combat zones was escalated as more men were committed to the conflict, and the helicopter force found itself under increasing attack from ground fire. The first response in the fifties had been to arm the then-prevalent Vertol H-21 with a light machine gun operated from the open door, but the first really effective countermeasures were taken in 1962 when the US Army's Utility Tactical Transport Helicopter Company was deployed. Its fleet of UH-1 Iroquois were fitted with 0.3 in machine guns and 2.75 in rockets to test the gunship principle. This development was taken still further in the purpose-built AH-1 HueyCobra gunship, described fully in Chapter 4.

The UH-1 became the chosen vehicle for the US Army's Air Cavalry – a mobile, maneuverable and well-armed group whose support, as at Ia Drang in October 1965, often proved crucial to the success of their ground-based counterparts. Lieutenant Colonel H. G. Moore, commander of the 1st Battalion of the 7th Cavalry, then commented: 'I have the highest admiration, praise and respect for the . . . UH-1D pilots and crews who ran a gauntlet of enemy fire

Previous page: A Bell UH-1 Huey of an Air Cavalry unit swoops to assist US troops in Vietnam.

Opposite, above: The twin-engined Model 212 was the civil equivalent to the UH-1N variant.

Opposite: The Bell 214, with 18-seat capacity, was the ultimate Huey spinoff.

The UH-1 proved the mainstay of the US helicopter operations in Vietnam. It served as a troop transport for up to 14 men (*main picture*), provided armed support when called in by ground forces (*inset right*) and gained an enviable reputation as a reliable casualty evacuation vehicle (*inset bottom*).

Left: Sikorsky's S-62 coupled the rotor and other systems of the S-55 with a T-58 turboshaft engine. It sold reasonably in the short term but made little lasting impact on the civil or military markets.

Below: Mil's twin-turbine Mi-8 seen here in Hip-E gunship configuration, was the Soviet response to Sikorsky's S-61.

time after time to help us . . . None were shot down and destroyed although most of them took hits.'

The battle he described lasted three days, during which time two Hueys were in fact downed through battle damage. They were airlifted to safety by Boeing Vertol CH-47 Chinook heavy lifters. In the seventies, however, the vulnerability of the helicopter to ground fire was multiplied by the advent in the North Vietnamese armory of the Soviet SA-7 Grail surface-to-air missile, effective against aircraft under 10,000 ft, and this to some extent negated the advances in gunship design and technology that had brought the AH-1 HueyCobra into play.

If turbine engines had given designs like the Sikorsky S-58 a new lease of life (as the Westland Wessex), then it seemed obvious that helicopters designed around the new power plants would boast even greater improvements in all-round performance. What was more, using two engines where only one would previously have been fitted provided greater safety levels, especially important over cities and on overwater flights.

Sikorsky, as ever, were in the forefront of developments with the S-61 Sea King. As its name suggested, it was a fully amphibious craft with a sealed, boat-section hull and outrigger floats to accommodate twin retractable mainwheel members; the tailwheel was fixed. Two General Electric T58 turboshafts, each of 1250 shp (later up-rated to 1400 shp), drove a five-bladed rotor to take advantage of the increased power available. The first Sea King flew on 11 March 1959, entering US Navy service two and one half years later with submarine hunter units VHS-3 at Norfolk, Virginia, and VHS-10 at Ream Field, San Diego.

The S-61, designated SH-3 in US armed forces service, had been intended to combine

the hunter and killer roles previously adopted by two piston-engined S-58s. The dipping sonar required for submarine detection was coupled with Doppler search radar and a radar altimeter, while up to 840 pounds of homing torpedoes and depth charges could be carried to finish the job. The hull proved roomy enough to encourage the development of utility transport (SH-3G) and VIP (VH-3A/D) variants, the latter serving with the US Executive Flight Detachment in Washington for Presidential duties. A fuselage stretch increased capacity to up to 28 passengers and resulted in the civil S-61L, equipped for land operation only. Yet a significant enough number of potential airline operators existed who required the S-61L to be re-amphibianised: British European Airways, for example, operated the S-61N, as it was designated, from Penzance

Right: A Canadian S-61 lands in the helicopter platform of the destroyer HMCS *Iroquis.* The S-61 is one of the largest shipborne helicopters in service.

Inset above right: Westland developed the S-61 design to provide the Sea King.

Above: Winner of the US Army's Light Observation Helicopter (LOH) competition in 1965 was the Hughes OH-6A Cayuse.

Left: Although an unsuccessful LOH contender, Fairchild Hiller put their OH-5A into production as the civil FH-1200.

Opposite top: Sikorsky's S-56/CH-54 Skycrane shown carrying a Universal Military Pod equipped as a surgical unit.

Opposite below: Mikhail Mil's Mi-10 Harke also carried its load under an abbreviated fuselage, but is pictured without any external cargo.

to the Scilly Isles west of England, while its flotation capability helped the S-61N become a favored offshore oil support type.

Sikorsky production ended in 1980, but the S-61 line was continued in Italy by Agusta under license. Westland in Britain had developed the type in the Sixties as the Sea King and this too remained in production in the eighties.

The US Air Force had borrowed a handful of SH-3s from the Navy in 1962 to supply radar units based offshore in the Atlantic – a mission profile, coincidentally, identical to that of oil rig support sorties. Convinced of the type's potential, the USAF requested certain changes to the basic design, most notably a hydraulically-opening rear fuselage door for the carriage of wheeled equipment, retractable tricycle undercarriage (the SH-3's watertight hull was retained) and an internal winch to handle other cargo. The emphasis was on self-sufficiency, with

an auxiliary power unit supplying power with the rotor at rest and completing a package that could operate irrespective of available ground facilities.

First deliveries of the S-61R/CH-3C were made at the end of 1963, the period of only six months from first flight emphasizing its easy development from the S-61/SH-3. The Coast Guard operated the type in the search and rescue role as the HH-3F Pelican, but it was the intermediate HH-3E that was to become the most famous mark of the family. With high-speed hoist, self-sealing fuel tanks, armor plating, retractable flight refueling probe and four-minigun armament, the Jolly Green Giants, as they were known because of their camouflage, carried out missions into North Vietnamese airspace to rescue aircrew with no little success.

The S-61/CH-3 was one of the first helicopters to investigate the possibilities of air-to-air refueling. On 1 July 1967, two S-61s

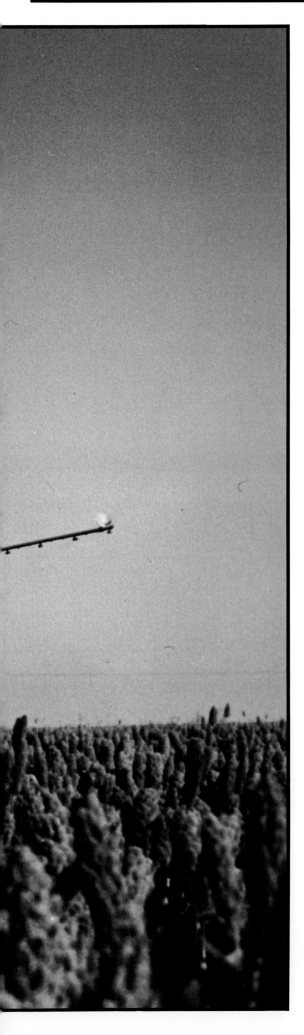

flying to the Paris Air Show made a non-stop crossing of the Atlantic – the first such crossing ever successfully completed by a helicopter – with the aid of nine in-flight refueling shots. The technique was often to be used to extend the type's range on operational missions, but one problem encountered was achieving a common speed between tanker aircraft and helicopter. Despite a creditable maximum speed of 166 mph, the SH-3 was obliged to refuel from propeller-driven aircraft, whose stalling speed was slower than that of a pure jet, or from sister helicopters 'buddy' fashion.

Both versions of the S-61 had in fact been beaten into the air by the single-engined S-62. Similar in appearance to the S-61, the S-62 leapfrogged its larger sister by utilizing the rotor, control and hydraulic systems of the S-55 with a de-rated T-58 turboshaft. At 730 shp, this gave 130 more horsepower than its predecessor's piston engine, yet its weight saving also promoted a considerable increase in payload. As the HH-52A, it replaced the H-34 (Sikorsky S-58) in Coast Guard Service, and was license-built by Mitsubishi in Japan, but was nowhere near as successful as the S-61 in the final analysis due to its smaller size.

Mikhail Mil's design bureau in the Soviet Union matched Sikorsky's domination of the Western medium transport field by flying the Mi-8 in 1961. At first glance a turbine-engined derivative of the ubiquitous Mi-4, its development took it along very much the same lines as the S-61 with twin Isotov turboshafts of 1500 shp apiece supplanting the prototype's single 2700 shp Sovloviev and a five-bladed rotor replacing the now-antiquated Mi-4 assembly previously used. Rear doors duplicated the Sikorsky S-61R's ease of loading, although it could plainly boast no capability for operation from water. The Mi-8, code-named Hip by NATO, went into production for the Warsaw Pact in 1967 and was subsequently delivered to some 20 countries worldwide.

One of the helicopter's most valued assets had always been its ability to airlift loads from inaccessible areas. Should the load prove too bulky to be accommodated, it might be underslung; yet a requirement obviously existed for a heavy lift helicopter, powered by new-technology turbine engines, which could lift a payload equal to its own empty weight. Once more Mil and Sikorsky were left to battle it out for world leadership, and both came up with similar ideas in the Mil Mi-10 Harke and Sikorsky S-64/CH-54 Skycrane.

The Mi-10 was rather larger than its rival, and had provision for 28 passengers in addition to its freight-carrying capabilities. Four large, stalky main undercarriage members protruded below the abbreviated fuselage, between which loads as large as a prefabricated building or motor coach could be carried. Sikorsky's Skycrane – first flown on

Left: The final LOH competitor was Bell's OH-4A, developed as the Jet Ranger. By the 1980s, it had proved the company's most successful helicopter since the Model 47. A crop spraying variant is pictured.

Inset far left: The high cost of Hughes' OH-6A led to the belated selection of the Jet Ranger, now re-designated OH-58A Kiowa, as the US Army's LOH for the 1970s.

Above: Igor Bensen's 'fun-to-fly' Gyro-Copters brought the autogiro back to prominence in the 1960s after a 30-year absence. Both factory and home-built examples have flown in some numbers.

treated – a major contributory factor in the majority of fixed-wing agricultural accidents – made it immediately popular, with types such as the Bell 47, Hiller UH-12 and Hughes 269 once more the leaders due to their low cost of acquisition and maintenance. Not only could the helicopter land and refuel/replenish its hoppers in an area no greater than the size of a tennis court, but the downwash of air from the rotor blades caused the underside – as well as the top leaves – of the foliage to be coated. The fitting of bolt-on spray arms rarely caused any problems either to the machine or to its aerodynamic properties, and these kits were soon widely available to users.

Many 'helicopter airlines' flourished briefly in the sixties, most American carriers being aided in their initial stages by government funding. When in 1966 the US government withdrew its subsidies to these operators, the airlines stepped in to try to maintain what was, to them, a useful service to their passengers. But the economics of operating regular services with less than 100 percent load factors were ultimately to prove prohibitive in the majority of cases. In Europe, Sabena of Belgium subsidised their rotary-wing 'feeder' operations from their more profitable fixed-wing routes, but finally admitted defeat and sold their fleet of Sikorsky S-58s to the armed forces in 1962.

The high costs associated with rotorcraft development have, as has already been noted, led to development proceeding along the most logical lines possible – the improvement and adaptation of existing designs and systems to produce a more effective product. Furthermore, funding for such research has most often become available from military sources, notably in the United States where success in design competitions frequently leads to substantial orders.

Little wonder, then, that the majority of notable civil helicopters have tended to result from such competitions – a spinoff process that has led to more than one 'winner' among the field. Such was the case with the US Army's Light Observation Helicopter competition, the specification for which was originally issued in 1960. A staggering 12 companies made submissions, from which three – Bell, Hiller and Hughes – were selected to produce five prototypes apiece. Trials began at Fort Rucker, Alabama, in November 1963 to determine the helicopter that could most nearly fulfill the many and varied roles of casualty evacuation, close support, photo reconnaissance, observation and light transport. To top all that, the machine had to possess a cruising speed of 120 mph, carry a payload of 400 pounds and have a four-seat capacity. Unsurprisingly, perhaps, it took 18 months to put the Bell OH-4A, Fairchild Hiller OH-5A and Hughes OH-6A through the evaluation process. Hiller's machine was eliminated, but put into production as the

9 May 1962, the year after Mil had unveiled his creation at the Tushino Air Display – was somewhat smaller and made use of the experience gained with the experimental S-60 between 1959 and 1961. It resembled nothing so much as a helicopter with a cockpit, backbone and tail boom but no fuselage, the intention being that the S-64 would straddle standardized pods or pallets of the kind commonly employed for freight.

Standard payload of the military CH-54 was a purpose built Universal Military Pod, intended for use as a troop carrier, communications center, surgical unit or command post. When pods were unavailable, ingenuity took over – one CH-54A lifted a van containing 90 personnel, all but the driver being troops carrying full combat equipment. Despite its obvious applications, however, the Skycrane was not ordered by any foreign service, and the handful of civil examples sold in the US represented the only non-US Army procurement of the type.

It was during the sixties that the helicopter defined certain tasks to be uniquely its own, while taking over others from the realm of fixed-wing aviation. Police work was one area in which the helicopter plainly excelled; with the addition of a loudhailer and searchlights, such basic machines as the Hughes 269 and Bell 47 were ideal aerial patrol cars, assisting as much with the apprehension of vandals and criminals as with reporting on traffic congestion. Hovering over a particular accident or traffic problem, a helicopter could direct operations by radio to clear the obstruction in the shortest possible time.

Crop spraying was another task that fell quite logically to rotorcraft. The helicopter's ability to fly at the low speeds required to provide an even coverage of the area to be

Above: Lockheed's experimental L-286 helped develop a rigid rotor system in the 1960s.

Far left: The Bölkow (MBB) Bö 105 brought the rigid rotor concept to commercial fruition.

Left: The Wallis WA 117 autogiro, fitted with a Vinten panoramic camera, was flown for profit not pleasure.

Opposite: A Sikorsky S-61/SH-3A of the US Navy demonstrates its dipping sonar, the most potent and flexible method of submarine detection yet devised.

Above: A Kaman Seasprite employs another sub-hunting tactic – flying a Magnetic Anomaly Detection 'bird.'

civil FH-1100. It achieved some success in this field, and was restored to production in the eighties as the F-1100. The Bell OH-4A was likewise discarded, but its manufacturers also announced that production would commence for the civil market. On 26 May 1965 the Hughes OH-6 Cayuse, an attractive egg-shaped craft, emerged victorious.

Performance-wise, the Cayuse was clearly a winner. It set 23 world records in the mid sixties, including a 2313-mile non-stop flight from California to Florida, a maximum sustained altitude in horizontal flight at 26,447 ft and speeds of up to 171 mph. The type was durable, too; one OH-6A in Vietnam was shot down and repaired no less than five times. But unit cost of the type proved to be higher than anticipated and this, together with delays in the production schedule, led to the US Army reopening the design competition in 1967. Bell's Model 206 JetRanger, a slightly larger version of the OH-4A, turned the tables to win – and, since orders for only 1434 Hughes OH-6As had been placed of the estimated requirement of some 4000, there had clearly still been much to compete for. The OH-58 Kiowa, as Bell's contender was designated, differed from its civil sister only in having a larger rotor and military avionics; it may not have had the Hughes' exciting performance despite sharing its 317 shp Allison turboshaft, but satisfied the Army minima. And, what was more, the JetRanger had meanwhile established itself

as one of the most popular and reliable corporate helicopters ever, with production lines at Fort Worth and in Italy, so costs were unlikely to prove a major problem.

Within four months of the first delivery in May 1969 the Kiowa was in action in Vietnam. Similar aircraft later saw service with 10 foreign air arms, while Hughes, who had continued manufacturing the OH-6 for the civil market as the Model 500, were loath to leave the export market to the mercy of its once-vanquished rival. By equipping it with self-sealing fuel cells and armor, infra-red exhaust suppressor, a quieter five-bladed rotor and other minor design changes, Hughes even produced a helicopter gunship 'on the cheap' which found favor with a growing number of air arms worldwide in the eighties as the Hughes 500M Defender.

The arrival of three such exceptionally capable helicopters on the civil market as spin-offs from the US Army's LOH competition inevitably damaged the sales prospects of the light sporting plane's rotary-wing equivalents. In the early sixties, it had seemed that a market might exist for high-performance, 'fun-to-fly' rotorcraft with two to three seats. Leaving aside the relative merits of fixed and rotary-wing flying from the pilot's viewpoint, economic factors – the cost of manufacture and operation – meant that a privately-owned helicopter remained well beyond the reach of the majority. Furthermore, individuals wealthy enough

to purchase one of these machines would probably expect it to double as an executive transport with the appropriate accommodation and baggage space.

Such considerations led to the eclipse of a number of exotic-looking craft such as the twin-rotor, shark-like Filper Beta, and also probably damaged the prospects of R. J. Enstrom's F-28 and N. O. Brantly's B-2. Enstrom's first prototype had been flown on 12 November 1960 and was an attractive three-seater with a gross weight of less than 2000 pounds (to put this in perspective, a light aircraft is defined as not exceeding 12,500 pounds). By the time deliveries began in the mid sixties, training and agricultural versions had been added to the range to stimulate sales, but success was only moderate. Nevertheless, the design was purchased and reinstated in production in the mid seventies as the turboshaft-powered Spitfire Mark 1A by the Pennsylvania-based concern of the same name.

N. O. Brantly's B-2 had taken seven years to reach production status after its first flight in February 1953. But Brantly, a former weaving machinery engineer, was very much a self-taught manufacturer who had flown his co-axial B-1 in 1946 with blades hinged six feet from the rotor shaft. The B-2 was considerably more conventional, with a teardrop-shaped fuselage accommodating two pilots at dual controls and a rudimentary skid undercarriage. Its gross weight of 1670 pounds all but qualified it as an ultra-light helicopter and, like the Enstrom F-28, it garnered valuable additional sales in the training and agricultural fields. Again in common with the Enstrom design, Brantly's B-2B was still to be found in small-scale production in the mid eighties, in this case by Hynes Helicopters in Oklahoma. The market for sporting helicopters had clearly found its own level.

The sixties saw the return of the autogiro, the development of which as a serious alternative to the helicopter had ended with the death of Don Juan de la Cierva in 1936. The man who put the autogiro back on the map was American Dr. Igor Bensen, formerly Chief of Research of the Kaman Company. He made no great claims for his design other than that it was cheap and easy to fly. His first experiments with 'gyro-gliders' towed behind a motorcar or motor boat led to the B-8M Gyro-Copter, a single-seat autogiro powered by a 72 hp piston engine. His Bensen Aircraft Corporation sold sets of plans (over 40,000 by the mid eighties), as well as completed aircraft, and provided the inspiration for many similar designs. The most refined of these was arguably the series created in Britain by Wing Commander Ken Wallis, who flew the first of his single-seaters in August 1961. These autogiros were subsequently to be seen fulfilling tasks as diverse as appearing in the *James Bond* movie series and assisting the police in an aerial search

for a buried murder victim. Although these machines were never made commercially available, Wallis concluded an agreement with W. Vinten Ltd., airborne reconnaissance specialists, to develop the type for civil and military applications in the eighties.

The design of Bölkow's Bö 105 in 1962 represented (West) Germany's real re-entry into the rotorcraft field it had dominated in the later inter-war years. And the new helicopter was very soon making a name for itself, being one of the first to use a rigid rotor. Although flight trials in early 1967 were initially carried out with a conventional rotor assembly, the rigid rotor had been tested successfully on a Sud Aviation Alouette II, and was fitted to the second prototype. Soon pictures of the Bö 105 looping, rolling and performing maneuvers more often associated with fixed-wing aircraft were to be seen in the aviation press. The fact that a rigid rotor could withstand negative G forces not only explained this phenomenon, but was also to have significant implications for 'nap of the earth' flight.

The rigid (or hingeless) rotor is one in which flapping and dragging are not permitted, the blades being cantilevered from the hub and capable of changes in pitch only. Its advantages include a high degree of stability and maneuverability, a greater center of gravity range and increased speeds, while the advantages of manufacture and maintenance are self-evident. The system was pioneered by the Lockheed CL-475, first flown at the end of 1959, and developed in that company's model 186/286 series, before being adopted by the German newcomers.

Bölkow had first tested the rotor extensively on a ground rig, but the experiment was all the more noteworthy in that the company had previously only flown one nontethered helicopter – the Bö 103 of 1961 – before embarking on the project. Nevertheless, the Bö 105 was a success despite a relatively high unit cost: West Germany's *Heeresflieger* (army air corps) ordered over 400, half as communications machines and half as missile-equipped tankbusters, while the Netherlands, Sudan, Nigeria and Philippines were other military customers. The type also enjoyed success in the civil field. Power plants were standardized at two 400 shp Allison turboshafts.

The helicopter at sea was now an established weapon of warfare, capable of detecting submarine movements by means of sonar 'dunked' while at the hover and destroying its enemy by means of depth charges or torpedoes. It could also provide an 'over the horizon' observation facility, replenish ships (either hovering or landed) by carrying supplies from a central stores vessel and provide a measure of protection for convoys outside the range of land-based air cover. And it also represented a welcome lifeline to ditched aircrew or seamen.

The requirements for successful ship-

Opposite above: Kamov's insect-like Ka-26 proved to be that design bureau's most successful and adaptable civil rotorcraft.

Opposite: The Ka-25 Hormone was the Soviet Navy's standard ASW helicopter for many years. Contra-rotating rotors meant a smaller fuselage length, and easier shipboard storage.

board operation were manifold: a folding tail and/or rotor assembly for ease of storage, castoring undercarriage to facilitate landing from any direction, all-weather navigation and stabilization systems to remain within safety limits and a strong structure to withstand the elements. The cost of converting a land-borne type to accommodate these features would normally have been prohibitive, a fact that tended to encourage the development of purpose-built naval helicopters.

The means by which the helicopter tracked down its submarine opponent were various. Most common was the sonobuoy, dropped into the water to send back any sounds and signals discerned beneath it. Less wasteful was the so-called 'dunking' sonar – a retractable sonobuoy dipped into the water from a hovering helicopter before being retrieved and deployed in another location. For this technique to be effective, sophisticated radar altimeters were developed to ensure that a steady hovering height was maintained during the maneuver, and computers often plotted the patterns flown for maximum efficiency of operation. Another method of detecting a submarine's presence was the magnetic anomaly detector which, as its name suggested, showed up any deviations in the sea's expected magnetic field. This method required a 'bird' to be towed on the end of a retractable cable behind the helicopter so that the readings obtained would not be affected by the presence of the helicopter itself.

One of the most diminutive anti-sub-

marine helicopters ever was developed by Agusta of Italy, a company which had cut its teeth on license production of the Bell 47 in the early fifties. When first flown in November 1965, it was the latest of a string of original designs which had begun with the A.103 of 1959 and included a giant three-engined 35-seater in the A.101G. The A.106 could not have been more different, a single-seater with a two-blade rotor driven by a 260 hp Turboméca-Agusta turboshaft. With two torpedoes underslung, it looked more like a pregnant grasshopper than a serious threat to submarines, yet was considered promising enough for a small production batch to be embarked aboard *Impavido* class ships, supplementing Agusta's larger license-built Bell and Sikorsky ASW types.

Paralleling the Westland Wasp and Kaman Seasprite, the helicopters most commonly deployed on board ship by the Western allies, was the Soviet Navy's Kamov Ka-25. Following its revelation at the Tushino display in 1961, the Hormone (as NATO code-named the type) was subsequently to be seen in ever-increasing numbers. The new type was more than four times as heavy as the Ka-18 already described, sharing its general layout and co-axial rotor configuration. Twin 900 shp Glushenkov turboshafts, each with its own fuel supply, provided an extra safety factor, while the radar, sonar and MAD equipment it carried was believed to be comparable with that of the West. Although compact in appearance due to its short tail boom and absence of tail rotor, the type was actually heavier than the Sikorsky S-58/Westland Wessex series. Unlike those helicopters, it was not usually employed in the submarine killer role, leaving the task to surface vessels even though an internal weapons bay was fitted. The Ka-25 was deployed aboard the carriers, cruisers and destroyers of the Soviet fleet in two versions – the sub-hunting Hormone-A and the radar picket and missile guidance Hormone-B.

Though Nikolai Kamov's family of co-axial rotorcraft were most often connected with the Soviet Navy, the mid sixties saw the appearance of an indubitably civil design, the Ka-26, from that very stable. Somewhat insect-like in appearance, the Ka-26 shared the attribute of the similar Kaman Huskie in that its engines, being out of the way of the cabin (the Ka-26's 325 hp Vedeneev piston units being podded either side), the entire fuselage was available for load carrying. In fact, the type was frequently to be seen with a chemical hopper in the cabin and spray booms for crop treatment fitted. By 1977, over 600 examples were active in 15 countries, while numerous examples had emulated the shipboard activities of their military sisters in the whaling, ice-breaking and fishing fields. Rather less successful was Kamov's most off-the-wall project, the Ka-22 Vintokryl. Russia's only known convertiplane, its two 5622 shp

Sovloviev turboshafts powered both rotors and propellers at the tips of its shoulder-mounted wing. It established a world speed record of 221.4 mph before returning to obscurity.

Sud Aviation's first tentative steps towards building a large transport helicopter were taken in conjunction with Sikorsky of the United States and Fiat in Italy, who collaborated on the rotor and transmission systems respectively. The result, the SA.321 Super Frelon, was a little larger than the Sikorsky S-61R, whose general layout it shared. Powered by three Turboméca Turmo turboshafts each developing 1550 shp, production Super Frelons were available in both land-based and amphibious versions. Israel was first to purchase the former in 1967, using the SA.321K as an assault helicopter for quick-reaction troop transport. In French service, the Super Frelon was more often seen as an anti-submarine helicopter, in which role its four-hour endurance and suitability for shipboard operation (boat hull, folding tail section) compensated for its large size.

Mikhail Mil's move into the turbine age was made on both a large and a small scale. The Mi-6 was undoubtedly considered more significant by observers since it had become, on its maiden flight in September 1957, the largest helicopter in the world. Its significance was as much geographical as mechanical, for one of the main aims of this joint military/civil project was to help exploit the potential of the Soviet Union's less accessible but no less potentially profitable regions. The military potential of the 26,000 pound payload of troops and/or armored vehicles was both obvious and equally important, and was graphically demonstrated at the Tushino Air Display in 1961. Six of these gigantic helicopters landed in two groups, one machine of each section disgorging a pair of artillery missiles and transporters, the others disembarking the crews and associated equipment to operate them.

The Mi-6 followed Western thinking in its choice of turbine engines and their positioning over the cabin. A considerable jump from the technology of the Mi-4 had been required, the Mi-6's gearbox and rotor head together weighing nearly twice its predecessor's internal payload.

In all-passenger configuration, the Mi-6 (NATO Hook) seated an airliner-load of 65, the power to lift them skywards being supplied to the massive 114 ft diameter five-bladed rotor by two 5500 shp Sovloviev turboshafts. The assistance of two variable-incidence winglets, attached to the fuselage above the main undercarriage struts, also proved useful, offloading 20 percent of the helicopter's weight in cruising flight. Maximum speed of the Mi-6 was in excess of 300 kmph (186 mph) – and, by becoming the first helicopter to exceed that figure, it won the Igor Sikorsky International Trophy in 1961.

Above: A Sud Aviation Super Frelon of France's Aéronavale unleashes an Exocet air-to-surface missile. The helicopter's usual mission is anti-submarine warfare.

Mil's other turbine-engined project could hardly hope to rival such a leviathan; indeed, the fact that it was a twin-turbine conversion of the Mi-1 could hardly hope to add to its interest. Yet the Mi-2 (Hoplite in the NATO codebook) was to prove rather more than a stop-gap measure. Firstly, its payload increased from three to eight persons in a fuselage redesigned to accommodate the two 400 shp Isotov engines above the cabin, their weight barely exceeding half that of the Mi-1's Ivchenko piston while developing fully 40 percent more power. Secondly, the type was put into series production in 1965 by the WSK-Swidnik (now PZL) aircraft factory in Poland, thus becoming the first and only Soviet-designed helicopter to be built *solely* outside its country of origin. And thirdly, when reimported, the type was adopted as the Soviets' main pilot and weapons training helicopter, in which role it served into the eighties. The type was also marketed in the US with indigenous Allison power plants as the Spitfire/PZL Taurus.

The antecedents of Sikorsky's S-65/H-53 Sea Stallion might have been confusing, but there was little doubt that the result was one of the West's most impressive heavy lift helicopters. Resembling a larger S-61R/H-3 in appearance, it was in fact a direct descendant of the S-64/CH-54 Skycrane, many of whose components it utilized. Its cargo-carrying ability was enhanced by rear-loading doors, winches and roller-track that facilitated the transport of such items as a $1\frac{1}{2}$ ton truck and trailer, a 105 mm howitzer or an Honest John missile. Like the H-3, it had a watertight hull, but eclipsed its smaller sister in length (67 ft 2 in, nearly 10 ft longer), rotor diameter (72 ft $2\frac{3}{4}$ in, 10 ft bigger) and power plant (two 2850 shp General Electric T64 turboshafts).

The S-65 first flew on 27 August 1962, deliveries of the production CH-53 to the USMC commencing four years later in September 1966. By the beginning of 1967, the type was operational in Vietnam, where the Marine Corps' aircraft were soon to be joined by the US Air Force's HH-53B. This featured uprated engine, jettisonable fuel tanks, equipment and armor similar to the HH-3E (including a retractable flight refueling probe) and armament. In this form, it served alongside the HH-3E in the Aerospace Rescue and Recovery Service. The

Above: Mil's mighty Mi-6, at the time of its introduction the world's largest rotorcraft.

Right: Re-engining the venerable Mi-1 with twin turbines resulted in the Mi-2, built under license in Poland by PZL.

Opposite: A Sikorsky CH-53 of the US Marine Corps demonstrates its lifting capabilities by picking up a Grumman EA-6 Prowler.

Right: Air-to-air refueling extends the range of this RH-53D Sea Stallion. Although fast, it could not refuel from a KC-135 jet tanker, hence the use of the propeller-driven KC-130F Hercules.

Inset far right: The imposing CH-53E Super Stallion, ultimate development of Sikorsky's S-61/ S-65 designs. The tail fin and rotor have been canted to offset the torque of a seven-bladed rotor while the enlarged sponsons hold extra fuel.

type was also adopted by the US Navy as its standard minesweeping helicopter, the RH-53D, designed to operate with equipment to detect and destroy all kinds of mechanical, acoustic and magnetic mines. The S-65 was also manufactured by VFW-Fokker in Germany for the Federal German Luftwaffe, 110 aircraft being assembled and/or manufactured there to add to an initial order for two fulfilled by Sikorsky.

The RH-53D Sea Stallions operate against mines in one of two ways: firstly, the helicopter can tow a sled-like device over the surface of the water in an attempt to explode magnetic or acoustic mines. The second is to cut the moorings of mines tethered to the sea bed by an explosive charge, leaving the disposal of the mine to surface ships once the weapon has bobbed into view. Four RH-53Ds were based aboard the transport carrier USS *Shreeveport* in the summer of 1984, sweeping the Red Sea for mines sown by an as-yet unknown power.

A more impressive development still, the three-engined S-65A/CH-53E Super Stallion, flew on 1 March 1974. Distinguishing feature

of the new mark was the tail fin and rotor canted 20 degrees to port to counter the increased torque of the seven-blade titanium and glassfiber rotor. The new engine/rotor combination promised to offer double the lifting potential of the CH-53 with an increase of only 50 percent in engine power. When the second prototype flew at an all-up weight of 74,500 pounds, it registered the highest gross weight of any helicopter outside the USSR.

The uses of the CH-53E seemed almost limitless, and included vertical onboard delivery, the removal of damaged aircraft from carrier decks (98 percent of Marine Corps aircraft can be carried underslung without having to be dismantled) and the support of mobile construction battalions. As a troop carrier, it could accommodate 55 persons, or could airlift 93 percent of a US Marine Division's combat items. Finally, an airborne mine countermeasures version was scheduled for delivery to the US Navy in 1986. With enlarged sponsons each holding 500 US gallons of extra fuel, endurance of this MH-53E variant could exceed 20 hours.

The seventies was to see the trend towards international collaboration, already established in the fixed-wing world, become even more prevalent. And it was not hard to see why – for the economics of rotorcraft development rivalled even those of modern jet fighters in their proportions. Speed and mobility required the separate but integrated development of turbine engines and rotor systems; multi-service orders often dictated amphibious capability as a basic requirement; while the helicopter's traditional vulnerability to ground fire was to exert an ever stronger influence on the designer. In Europe, Aérospatiale (né Sud) of France and Britain's Westland Helicopters, who had separately begun to challenge the Sikorsky/Bell rotorcraft monopoly with their own designs, resolved to develop new types together in the seventies. Signed on 22 February 1967, the agreement predated the tri-nation Panavia Tornado fighter program, and was to prove no less successful.

The agreement covered three designs: two, the SA.330 Puma and the SA.341 Gazelle, would proceed under French design leadership, the third was Westland's WG.13 Lynx. The Puma was intended to provide a medium transport helicopter in the Wessex bracket, while the single-engined Gazelle and twin-engined Lynx bade fair to replace the Alouette II and Scout/Wasp series in their respective countries of origin. Additional export sales were contemplated for this new family of helicopters, perhaps the largest development program launched outside the United States at the time of its inception.

The SA.330 Puma bore an obvious family resemblance to the SA.321 Super Frelon, of which it was roughly two-thirds the size and, appropriately, possessed two of the Frelon's three Turboméca Turmo engines. Among its design features was a semi-retractable sponson-mounted undercarriage for emergency water operation, independent hydraulic systems and dual controls. The prototype flew on 15 April 1965, and impressed enough to scoop the Royal Air Force's requirement for a new turbine-powered tactical transport helicopter to supplant the Wessex. The last pre-production aircraft was modified to feature an external hoist and an internal cargo handling sling, two of the RAF's requirements, and the first Westland-built Puma flew in November 1970. The type became operational in the UK in the following year, French army aviation (ALAT) having accepted their first Pumas in March 1969.

Around 686 Pumas had been delivered by early 1983, with operators in some 46 countries. Production by then had switched to the AS.332 Super Puma with more powerful Turboméca Makila engines, improved landing gear and rotor systems, and this new mark quickly found favor in both the military and civil fields. Bristow Helicopters,

Previous page: A UH-60 Black Hawk of the US Army overflies the Pyramids during a joint US-Egyptian exercise.

Right: Aérospatiale's collaboration with Westland started with the Puma. Ordered by the armed forces of both France and Britain, the type was further developed as the AS.332 Super Puma (pictured) for the military and civil markets.

Inset far right: The Gazelle was covered by the same agreement of 1967, and has since proved an equal success. Its ducted fan or *fenestron* tail rotor provides an original recognition feature.

major British operators of offshore oil support helicopters, ordered 35 examples with 19-seat interiors. The type was also built under license in Indonesia by the state-owned Nurtanio concern.

The second of Sud Aviation's projects covered by the Anglo-French agreement was the SA.341 Gazelle. Like the Puma, this was to be assembled on both sides of the Channel, but was significantly smaller than its 18-seat sister. The SA.340, as it was first designated, had originally been conceived as the Project X 300 to meet a French Army light observation helicopter requirement similar to the US Army's Hughes OH-6A. The concept borrowed greatly from the Alouette II – so much so that the prototype, which flew on 7 April 1967, shared its Astazou engine and transmission system with that helicopter, as well as an Alouette III tail rotor. Yet production Gazelles were to differ in at least two important respects – the three-blade rotor was semi-articulated, with the mast and head forming a single unit, while the tail rotor was a shrouded fan or *fenestron* (literally 'fan-in-fin').

Nimble and extremely swift with a maximum speed approaching 200 mph, the Gazelle was selected to equip all three UK armed services, fulfilling the observation role with the Army Air Corps and the training function with the Fleet Air Arm and Royal Air Force. With the British Army, the Gazelle replaced the ageing Westland-built Bell 47G-2 Sioux, which had previously been carrying out the observation, reconnaissance, communications and forward air control tasks. The French army used the type for anti-tank operations.

Over 1000 Gazelles had been sold by the mid eighties, when the type was operating in at least 36 countries. Its popularity was boosted in 1975 when it became the first helicopter in the world to be certified for single-pilot operation under Instrument Flight Rules (IFR) Category I conditions, thanks to the combination of a British Sperry flight director and French SFENA servo-dampers. It was later cleared for IFR Cat II conditions with a ceiling of 100 ft and forward visibility of 1200 ft, further emphasising its enviable flying characteristics.

The final project of the international trio was the Westland Lynx, whose twin-engined multi-purpose specification immediately suggested maritime operations. The first of no less than 13 prototypes made its maiden flight on 21 March 1971, powered by a pair of 750 shp Rolls Royce Gem turboshafts, and in June 1972 a later aircraft set a speed record over a 25 km course of 199.9 mph (321.7 kmph). Performance and maneuverability were well up to expectation – and, although operational service trials were not to be concluded until 1977, it was clear long before then that this capable helicopter would form the backbone of the British forces' helicopter fleet for some years to come.

Right: Most recent of the Anglo-French rotorcraft collaborations was the Westland Lynx. A Royal Navy Lynx is here secured to the helicopter platform of the destroyer HMS *Birmingham* in rough seas.

German-based British Army Air Corps squadrons were the first to employ the Lynx operationally, teaming units of TOW missile-equipped tankbusters with squadrons of observation/forward air control Gazelles in the late seventies. 1984 saw the first flight of the Lynx 3, the design's ultimate gunship variant claimed to be Europe's most potent anti-armor helicopter.

The shipborne Lynx variant was soon to prove its worth also. Differing from its Army counterpart in having a four-wheel undercarriage (the nosewheels being mounted in a castoring tandem unit), it boasted a comprehensive radar and sonar package. Torpedoes, depth charges and air-to-surface missiles were among the armament options. Although the land-based Lynx received no orders from the French services, the naval variant was acquired to replace the ageing Sikorsky S-58s and the single-engined Alouette IIIs of the French Navy. Other countries to avail themselves of this advanced shipboard helicopter included Argentina, Brazil, Egypt, Denmark, Norway and Qatar.

The helicopter's value in warfare had been established from its first use in Korea as a casualty evacuation vehicle. Given undefended airspace, a helicopter could often penetrate behind enemy lines to retrieve aircrew or infantry. The next stage in Vietnam had been the deployment of 'aerial cavalry', troop carriers such as the Bell UH-1 Iroquis to infiltrate men and materiel where they might be able to use the advantage of surprise.

Such sorties, however, could rarely claim immunity from attack, at least from ground small-arms fire. And with the helicopter's traditional vulnerability to just such 'nuisance-value' action, the advent of hand-held anti-aircraft missile launchers and the like clearly demanded some form of self-defense. As previously recounted, the initial response was to arm examples of the UH-1 with machine guns and air-to-surface rockets, these being arrayed along each side of the fuselage. Bell, however, elected to redesign the battle-proven UH-1 airframe as a private venture to provide a more potent and significantly less vulnerable support helicopter for use in Vietnam, and the result was the Model 209, better known as the AH-1 HueyCobra.

The HueyCobra may have retained part of the designation and the familiar 'Huey' nickname acquired by its predecessor when first designated HU-1, but little save the tail assembly exhibited further common ground. The narrow (3ft 2 in) cross-section was achieved by seating the two crew members in tandem – and, as if to underscore the designers' priorities, the pilot was seated *behind* the gunner. Nose armament of two 7.62 mm Miniguns in a swiveling turret was augmented by rockets carried amidships in multi-tube launchers on the HueyCobra's stub wings. Later options were to include

grenade launchers and Hughes TOW air-to-surface missiles.

The firepower packed by this new and exciting gunship was quickly evident even before its first flight on 7 September 1965, while its performance – it had retained the UH-1's engine, rotor and transmission system – permitted faster speeds and longer missions. What was more, its relatively low unit cost and proven mechanical systems were to sound the death knell for the Lockheed AH-56, winner of the recent Advanced Aerial Fire Support System design competition. A sophisticated compound helicopter capable of speeds of up to 242 mph, the AH-56 Cheyenne proved too costly to proceed with, and the AH-1 was the beneficiary. Known as the 'Whispering Death' to the Vietcong, the HueyCobra proved the design concept time and again, delivering its warload with accuracy and proving a difficult target for ground gunners.

The US Marine Corps approached Bell to design a twin-engined HueyCobra variant, the reliability factor for overwater operation making this configuration especially attractive. The result was the AH-1J Sea-Cobra, basically similar to its predecessors save for its 1800 shp Pratt & Whitney Air-

Opposite: The threat of ground fire was initially countered by arming UH-1 crew members (*main picture*) and fitting rocket pods (*inset top*).

Above: Bell's next response was to redesign the UH-1 to provide a difficult target for ground marksmen – the result was the AH-1 Huey Cobra.

MIL MI-24 HIND-E

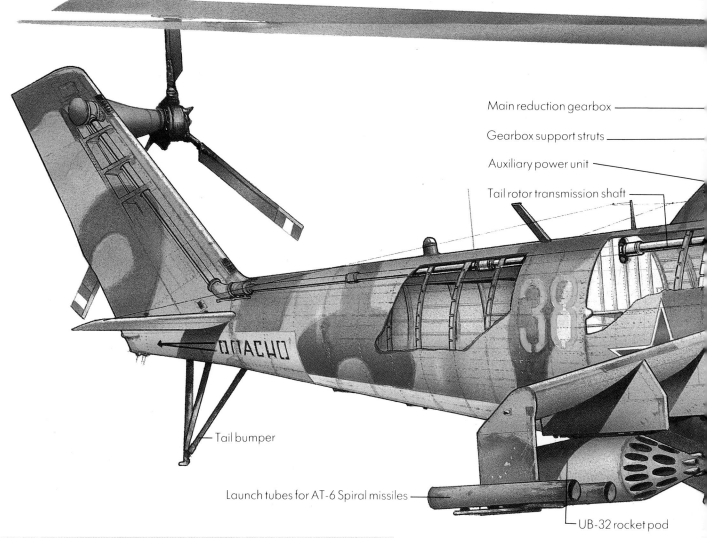

Main reduction gearbox

Gearbox support struts

Auxiliary power unit

Tail rotor transmission shaft

Tail bumper

Launch tubes for AT-6 Spiral missiles

UB-32 rocket pod

craft of Canada T400 twin turboshaft and the strengthening needed to counteract the increased torque acting upon the rear fuselage. An order for 202 similar aircraft came in 1972 from Iran, while an improved Sea-Cobra, the AH-1T, was the subject of follow-up USMC orders.

Ever mindful of the fate of the AH-56 Cheyenne program that had given the HueyCobra its chance, Bell made strenuous attempts to update the AH-1's design for possible service into the next century, coming up with the optimistically titled Cobra 2000. Based on the US Army's AH-1S, it would sport the improved Hughes TOW 2 ASM, 20 mm cannon and rockets, laser fire control and night vision sensors. The Bell Model 412's four-bladed main rotor would also be adopted, to be powered by an uprated Avco Lycoming engine.

The Soviet Union's definitive helicopter gunship was to take a somewhat different form. On first observation in 1973, the Mil Mi-24 Hind appeared an attempt to combine the gunship and assault helicopter roles – and, while the size dictated by the latter requirement plainly compromised the minimum-profile and high maneuverability phil-

Oil cooler

Isotov TV3-117 turboshaft engine

Intake debris extractors

Pilot's seat

Weapons systems officer's seat

Fuel tanks

Seating for 8 fully armed troops

Door lower segment incl. boarding step

Low pressure tyres

Radar director pod

Twin barrel externally mounted 23mm GShL-23 cannon

osophy adopted by Bell's AH-1, the result could not be ignored for its sheer firepower. Guns, guided missiles and unguided rockets in pods dealt with almost any contingency, while a 12-troop capacity was a considerable bonus. The Mi-24 employed the Mi-8's engines and transmission systems with a smaller airframe and rotor, but with both fuselage and rotor diameter measuring 56 ft, the result was indisputably bulky and unmaneuverable. The Hind-D variant noted in 1975 adopted certain improvements to airframe and armament, such as a heavily protected tandem-crew cockpit and a four-barrel 20 mm gun in the nose.

Hind's versatility was apparent in the Soviet invasion of Afghanistan, where its multi-mission capability made it ideal for operations against a poorly armed and organized enemy by Western standards.

Although there was some indication that the lack of such necessary refinements as infra-red suppressors on the engine exhausts would render Hind vulnerable to the West's state of the art weaponry, there is little doubt that the helicopter's size and fire-power would make it a feared adversary in Western skies. The Soviet *Red Star* reported that 'The correlation between tank and helicopter losses is 12:1 or even 19:1 in the helicopter's favor.' With the later Hind-E variant adding laser-designated AT-6 Spiral missiles to the wire-guided AT-2s already carried by Hind-D, that already impressive test ratio could only improve.

The near coincidence of two major US service design competitions in the early and mid seventies was to present Sikorsky with an opportunity to sweep the board of orders for a twin-turbine military helicopter of the

Left: UH-1E (nearer the camera) and an AH-1J Sea Cobra of the US Marines.

Left: Sikorsky's SH-60 Sea Hawk with torpedo armament. Above the torpedo are the hatches for dispensing sonobuoys.

Above: The Hind-E variant of Mil's impressive Mi-24 attack helicopter swings into action.

Opposite above: The SH-60B SeaHawk variant of Sikorsky's Black Hawk prepares to land on board ship. Note the haul-down system in operation.

Opposite bottom: Bell's sophisticated Model 222 was specifically designed for civil operation.

Bell 'Huey' class to serve until the end of the century. The S-70/H-60A Black Hawk was Sikorsky's submission for the US Army's UTTAS (Utility Tactical Transport Aircraft System) requirement, being selected in 1972 to run against the Boeing Vertol Model 179/H-61. The two competitors were both of conventional configuration, powered by a pair of 1500 shp General Electric T700 turboshafts, the most obvious difference being the S-70's tailwheel undercarriage (for speed of landing under fire) and canted tail surface and rotor.

Evaluation began in early 1976, and after seven months Sikorsky's design was declared the winner. Two years previously, the US Navy had decided to seek a successor for the Kaman SH-2F Seasprite which had been fulfilling the interim Light Airborne Multi Purpose System (LAMPS) role in ever-uprated versions. Both UTTAS contenders were evaluated, and the decision reached was the same as that of the Air Force – the Sikorsky S-70. Designated SH-60B SeaHawk in navalized form, the type's wheelbase was foreshortened by some 46 percent for ease of shipboard landing, while folding rotor blades and tailplane, reduced armor, an in-flight refueling capability and a comprehensive maritime avionics fit were also introduced.

Just over 1100 examples of the basic Black Hawk were expected to be ordered by the US Army up to and including the fiscal year 1990. That total included 77 EH-60A aircraft which, as their Electronic prefix suggested, carried ECM gear in the form of Quick Fix II communications jamming equipment and were distinguishable by their array of external aerials. The EH-60B was an altogether more complex option with a retractable rotating underbelly scanner to monitor the movement of enemy ground forces on the battlefield. Though the first of eight prototypes flew in February 1981, problems with the equipment and escalating cost caused

the project – and the proposed order of 70 helicopters – to be shelved.

Among the Black Hawk's many attributes was numbered an outstanding ability to survive under fire, the type being the first tactical transport helicopter to boast built-in tolerance to small arms fire (in both fuselage *and* rotor) and some resistance to anti-aircraft projectiles of larger caliber. A transatlantic ferry capacity (courtesy of extra tankage carried on stub-wing attachment points) freed Black Hawk from having to rely on fixed-wing transport from US bases to a possible European battleground and plainly enhanced the type's operational flexibility: Hellfire air-to-ground missiles could also be carried on the same stub wings, but normally remain the preserve of the Hughes AH-64A advanced attack helicopter. Nevertheless, tankbusting is one role that the Black Hawk could quite conceivably add to its many accomplishments – with export customers if not the US Army.

In Europe, Aérospatiale faced the seventies in the knowledge that their world-beating duo, the Alouette II and III, were unlikely to end the decade as marketable products. Their planned replacements were designated AS.350 Ecureuil (Squirrel) and SA.360 Dauphin (Dolphin) and first flew on 27 June 1974 and 2 June 1972 respectively.

The ten-passenger Dauphin borrowed the (admittedly developed) Astazou turboshaft from the Alouette II and the *fenestron* shrouded-fan tail rotor from the Gazelle, but the six-seat Ecureuil looked a new shape indeed. It wisely modified its name (to Astar) for the American market, where it more significantly exchanged its 641 hp Turboméca Arriel turboshaft for a home-produced 615 shp Avco Lycoming LTS 101 unit. By 1983, some 1015 examples were flying in 32 countries, including 12 pilot training aircraft with the Royal Australian Air Force. The emphasis in design had been on low noise and low costs, priorities which obviously paid off. A twin-engined AS.355 Ecureuil 2/Twinstar was developed with 425 shp Allison turboshafts, its greater safety margins making it especially popular with oil company fleets.

If the lines (and, indeed, the power plant) of the Ecureuil seemed unusually American for a Sud Aviation/Aérospatiale rotorcraft, the Dauphin was a different proposition altogether. The prototype ten-seat SA.360C Dauphin had set three class speed records just under one year after first flight, the most impressive being a speed of 193.9 mph (312 kmph) over a 3 km course. Yet its makers clearly thought there to be room for improvement, and so it proved: the first development was the replacement of the 1050 shp Astazou turboshaft with two smaller (680 shp) Arriel units, the resulting helicopter being designated SA.365C Dauphin 2.

Then came the major breakthrough in the

shape of the SA.365N Dauphin 2, which, despite the similarity in appearance and designation, retained only 10 percent component commonality with the SA.365C. First flown on 31 March 1979, its construction was, to say the least, unusual. Composites of glassfiber and such substances as Kevlar, Nomex and Rohacell made up 20 percent of the structure, while carbon fiber played a major part in the rotor construction. A light alloy/Nomex sandwich made up some 35 percent of the fuselage structure, while a retractable undercarriage and larger tail surfaces provided major external recognition points to distinguish this addition to the Dauphin line.

The rotor system, too, was different, replacing the standard blade hinges by a single rubber-steel sandwich ball joint. The result of Aérospatiale's labors was soon apparent when the first production aircraft set Paris-London-Paris (round trip and individual leg) speed records in February 1980: the Paris-London leg was flown at an average speed of 200.03 mph. While the Arriel turboshafts had now been uprated to 710 shp (as compared to the 680 shp of former versions), this was still remarkable.

The Dauphin's commercial success, however, was already assured. At the 1979 Paris Air Show, it had been announced that the US Coast Guard had awarded Aérospatiale a contract for 90 helicopters to perform the Short Range Recovery (SRR) task from the service's ship and shore bases. The HH-65 Dolphin, as the type was to be known in USCG service, differed from the SA.365N by having American power plants (two 680 shp Avco Lycoming turboshafts) as well as other equipment of US manufacture, bringing the cost of American components to about 60 percent of the total. Aérospatiale's willingness to bow to political expediency in this way helped the Dauphin become one of the few French aircraft to be bought by the US forces, its only postwar contemporary being the Dassault Falcon. Further orders came from Saudi Arabia – 24 Dauphins to serve as search and rescue and radar-equipped anti-ship helicopters – Ireland, who ordered five for fishing surveillance, and China, with whom a license-manufacturing deal was concluded in July 1980. Chinese production machines carried the designation Zhi-9 Haitun, the name being a literal translation of dolphin.

The American and Saudi Arabian orders necessitated the installation of highly sophisticated radar and communications systems. The American option, manufactured by Rockwell Collins, included a data link transmitting information on speed, position, wind conditions and fuel state to ship or shore and a Northrop infra-red search sensor. The Saudi anti-ship Dauphin carried the Agrion 15 nose radar derived from that of the Breguet Atlantic maritime patrol aircraft to locate targets for its four AS.15

Above: Although more often seen in civilian garb, the Agusta A 109A was employed by Argentina in the Falklands War. This example was captured by the British and now serves with the SAS.

Opposite: Aérospatiale's Dauphin makes use of much composite material to save weight, and the benefits this has conferred on performance have boosted sales considerably.

Inset opposite: The Aérospatiale Ecureuil 2 is known as the Twinstar when marketed in the United States where this example is pictured.

air-to-surface missiles carried on fuselage outriggers. All this made the Dauphin one of the most capable 'off the shelf' military helicopters of the eighties, setting the seal of success on Aérospatiale's seventies efforts to reproduce the Alouette family's earlier impact on the rotorcraft world.

While Aérospatiale could rely on the loyalty of their former Sud Aviation customers as a sound commercial base for new designs, a European competitor initially found its own twin-turboshaft multi-role helicopter took rather longer to win worldwide acceptance. Despite a history dating back to 1907, and a postwar record of manufacturing Bell and Sikorsky rotorcraft under license for the European market, Agusta of Italy had enjoyed only limited success with its own designs. The diminutive A.106 torpedo helicopter described elsewhere had made a limited impression but attracted no orders from outside its country of origin, and it was not until the advent of the A.109A that the company made an international mark. Even so, it was not until some years following the type's first flight on 4 August 1971 that the design made inroads into the international market, the breakthrough coming on its certification for single-pilot operation in Instrument Flight Rules conditions in early 1977.

By mid 1983, some 200 examples had been delivered. The A.109A had a particularly high performance for a seven-seat general executive helicopter, its maximum speed being 193 mph, and thus provided a 'step up'

for corporate owners already familiar with Agusta's license-built AB.206 JetRanger. An experimental A.109 was flown in 1984 with twin Turboméca Arriel turboshafts (replacing Allison units) in order to improve the levels of 'hot and high' performance demanded by Middle Eastern operators, while specialized attack, electronic countermeasures and naval variants were under development. The options open to police customers of the A.109 graphically demonstrated the helicopter's role in controling civil disturbance: 360-degree radar, loudspeakers, rescue hoist, stretcher/first aid kit, radar altimeter and smoke grenades were among the equipment on offer.

With European manufacturers meeting such success, the US 'big two' were quick to follow. When first announced in April 1974, the Bell Model 222 was claimed by its makers to be the first commercial light twin-engined helicopter to be built in the United States. It flew for the first time on 13 August 1976 and, although its twin 684 shp Avco Lycoming turboshafts made it perhaps an expensive helicopter for its eight-place layout compared with Bell's other excellent designs, it found favor with the ubiquitous oil-rig service fleets and, notably, London's Metropolitan Police. They took delivery of two Model 222 helicopters in 1980 and 1981, described at the time as 'the most sophisticated police helicopters in the world'. A Model 222, delivered to Omniflight Helicopters on 18 January 1981, was the 25,000th Bell rotorcraft to be built.

5 THE EIGHTIES AND BEYOND

So what of the helicopter's future? At least commentators of the eighties can be sure that the helicopter *has* a future, something that seemed in doubt as recently as World War II. Since then, it has successfully become a familiar part of modern life in so many different spheres that most people take it for granted – testimony indeed to its success.

Two factors in particular have been instrumental in putting the helicopter firmly on the aviation map. The first is its use in war as troop carrier, anti-submarine and surface vessel defender, air ambulance, aircrew and airframe retriever, heavy lifter and – perhaps most importantly – as a gunship and armament platform. The second is the increasing emphasis on exploiting the world's natural resources: oil, gas, minerals. As these resources are expended, exploration takes man into ever more inaccessible and inhospitable areas, where the modern all-weather helicopter can be of immeasurable assistance.

The helicopter's role on the battlefield has inevitably been shaped and molded by the experience of Vietnam, where more rotorcraft were employed than ever before. The US Army order of battle latterly included no less than seven distinct types: Bell AH-1 (gunship), Bell UH-1 (troop transport, medevac, command 'copter), Hughes OH-6 (light high-speed reconnaissance), Bell OH-58 (patrol and target acquisition), Sikorsky HH-3 (aircrew recovery), Sikorsky CH-54 (heavy lifter) and Boeing Vertol CH-47 (troop transport, forest clearance). The advantages of combining the various roles into fewer different types are obvious, and it was with this in mind that the US Army framed its LHX program, which foresaw a requirement for 5-7000 multi-purpose helicopters to replace the UH-1, AH-1, OH-6 and OH-58. It seemed possible that this might utilize the advancing blade concept (ABC) being tested by the Sikorsky S-69, but more likely that it would take the form of a developed family of helicopters sharing the same power plants and systems. Hughes were developing their AH-64 Apache with this aim in view in the mid eighties.

Vietnam, of course, is unlikely to form the battleground of any future major confrontation. As attention had focused on the European theater, so a complex equation of tanks, helicopters and aircraft evolved around the theory that a tank offensive was likely to play a major part in any conventional (that is non-nuclear) conflict to come. Deployment of the USAF's specialist Fairchild A-10 Thunderbolt II, for example, was intended to counter the imbalance in armor favoring the Warsaw Pact.

No matter how extensive the fighter cover under which it operated, however, the slow-flying Thunderbolt II would prove particularly vulnerable to surprise attack from air-to-air missile-equipped helicopters firing from close range, having appeared from camouflaged positions. Significantly the SA-7 Grail, normally a hand-held SAM, has been reported as being among the armament sported by Mil's mighty Mi-24 Hind-D, possibly with this very fact in mind. The US Army hoped the previously-mentioned LHX would counter this threat, but by the time it was scheduled to enter service the Soviets seemed certain to have added their own new breed of mobile 'helicopter fighter' to their armory in the shape of the Mil Mi-28 Havoc. Little was known about this newcomer in at the time of writing except that it was broadly comparable to the AH-64.

In addition to helicopters fighting their own private wars above the battlefield, the tankbusting helicopter had come into its own. Whereas the AH-1 HueyCobra gunship grew out of a need to minimize the dangers from ground fire to other main force helicopters, the helicopter's mission against the tank had evolved primarily from rapid advances in air-to-surface missile technology. In many respects, these advances had leapfrogged the airframes in which they have been flown, leading to the situation where an 'old-technology' helicopter such as the Aérospatiale (Sud Aviation) Alouette III suddenly became a cheap and effective tankbuster with little more than 'bolt-on' modifications.

One unexpected offshoot from this was the appearance of several species of 'off the peg' tankbusters – civil helicopters armed to the teeth and offered to Third World countries as their own 'cut-price Cobra'. Hughes made good the shortfall in OH-6 production for the US Army, for example, by pitching its civil Model 500 as the Model 500M Defender. Self-sealing fuel tanks, a coat of army-surplus camouflage paint and a host of missile, torpedo and gun options have seen Israel, Argentina and Japan join the queue. Bell's Texas Ranger derivative of their best selling Model 206 hoped to emulate its rival's performance as the eighties progressed. That both types started life in the early sixties as competitors in the US Army's Light Observation Helicopter competition spoke as much for the weapons they carried as for their own inherent design longevity.

Early examples of air-launched anti-tank missiles, such as the Aérospatiale AS.11, were adapted from surface-to-surface weapons. Like many of its successors, it operated on the principle of wire guidance, impulses from the gunner's joystick control being transmitted through trailing wires to be converted into correcting electrical signals to the missile's control surfaces. The larger AS.12 reduced the gunner's task merely to tracking the target with his sight, an infrared sensor automatically correcting the missile's course: this system was known as TCA (*TéléCommande Automatique*).

Similar to (but smaller and faster than) the

AS.12 was Hughes' BGM-71 TOW missile, first tested in action in Vietnam in 1972 when two Bell UH-1B helicopters destroyed 62 targets between them in a single action. The missile derived its acronym from its Tube-launched, Optically-tracked and Wire-guided function and proved an extremely capable weapon, its gyro-stabilized sight ensuring that the adverse effects of vibration and movement on accuracy were minimized. Night use was made possible by replacement of the visual control system by a FLIR (Forward-Looking Infra Red) sight with a thermal imaging sensor. An improved TOW with more effective 5-inch armor-penetrating warhead was designed and built as a stop-gap before the heavier and more powerful TOW 2 brought the missile back up to date. TOW was effective at ranges of 12,000 feet, and was carried by a large range of helicopters like the Bell AH-1, MBB Bö 105, Westland Lynx, Hughes 500M and military derivatives of the Agusta A.109.

Europe's major eighties contribution to the anti-tank helicopter's armament was HOT, Euromissile's High subsonic, Optically guided, Tube-launched weapon developed jointly by France's Aérospatiale and MBB of West Germany. It was similar in many respects to the Hughes TOW, being wire guided in response to an optical sight and having a two-stage propellant. The Venus system permitted night firing and was usual-ly mounted in a rotatable nose scanner. Its carriers included the Bö 105M, Aérospatiale Dauphin 2, Aérospatiale Gazelle and Westland Lynx.

The Lynx was also the vehicle for the British Aerospace Sea Skua, a two-stage radar-guided missile intended for use against patrol craft and other small vessels. Rockwell's AGM-114 Hellfire (HELicopter launched, Fire and Forget) was, as its full name suggested, a different system altogether to the wire-guided TOW, HOT and AS.12, yet its importance to helicopter warfare in the future could not be underestimated. With helicopter gunships likely to clash in the airspace over the battleground, their ability to press home individual attacks with wire-guided weaponry will be further reduced. The advantage of a missile that could be fired and guided automatically to the target while the helicopter that fired it made good its escape was therefore obvious. The method selected was laser designation, which relies upon a laser beam locked onto the target either from the launch helicopter, or from equipment on the ground or in another aircraft. The missile's guidance system seeks out the reflected laser light from the target, to which it is thereby guided.

Although Hellfire was tested with the Sikorsky H-60 Black Hawk and even the smaller Bell AH-1 HueyCobra, its intended vehicle was one designed to take the gun-

Above: The ominous Hughes AH-64A gunship lifts off. Its nose-mounted sights and sensors are clearly visible, along with Hellfire missiles on the stub wings.

Right: This German army Bölkow (MBB) Bö 105 sports six HOT anti-tank missiles.

Far right: A Royal Navy Lynx armed with four Sea Skua anti-ship missiles.

Inset below: A prototype Lynx pictured with Hellfire missiles.

Main picture: A TOW missile is launched from a British Army Air Corps Lynx.

ship and its associated technology into a new dimension – the Hughes AH-64.

The US Army Design Competition for an Advanced Attack Helicopter (AAH) for the eighties took place in 1976 and was contested by the Hughes AH-64 and Bell's AH-63. The aim was to find a two-seat gunship capable of surviving in a front-line environment and undertaking missions in all weathers and visibilities: a step up from the HueyCobra in both size and sophistication.

Hughes' prototypes began the evaluation of the sophisticated fire control systems just over a year after the AH-64's selection was announced in December 1976. With such onboard technology at risk, every means possible was considered to enhance survivability. Hughes' own 'Black Hole' infra-red suppressor system, for instance, diffused (and thus cooled) the gas exhaust from the engine to make it more difficult for a missile's infra-red detection system to lock onto it. The main rotor blades and fuel tank were designed to sustain strikes from 23 mm shells (a standard Soviet caliber) without critical damage, while the chance of crew survival in the event of a crash at 42 ft per second was estimated, through testing, at 95 percent.

The pilot and co-pilot/gunner sat in the now-accepted tandem seating arrangement, with the gunner occupying the forward position. Two systems assisted the crew in their task: the Target Acquisition and Designation Sight (TADS) and Pilot's Night Vision Sensor (PNVS), both mounted independently in the nose. The former incorporated a TV camera and laser rangefinder as daylight aids, turning to an infra-red sight for night targeting. The PNVS sensor operated via an electronics unit in the avionics bay, beaming to the pilot on a helmet monocle in front of one of his eyes: airspeed, altitude and heading were also superimposed in the manner of a head-up display to obviate the need to look down at instruments. This latter system permitted 'nap-of-the-earth' flight in darkness or poor conditions at low altitude both within and outside the battle area.

The 'nap of the earth' flying so often referred to in the context of modern combat helicopters is the rotorcraft's only defense against detection by radar. Hugging the earth's contours at a height of mere feet above the countryside, it thereby maintains the element of surprise over ground forces and armor. The rigid-rotor concept has much to do with the development of this kind of flying, since its simplified rotor mechanism can tolerate the negative g forces encountered when, say, the pilot pushes the nose down after climbing over a belt of trees. A conventional 'mobile' rotor assembly would render such maneuvers hazardous, if not impossible.

The Soviet response to the AH-64 may well beat it onto the battlefield. Although little is presently known of their proposed

fighter helicopters, it is fairly certain that the missiles they will carry will be among those already known to NATO.

Soviet helicopter missile development has, perhaps predictably, paralleled that of the West, with a wire-guided unit (AT-3 Sagger) and a laser designated fire and forget system (AT-6 Spiral) available. Other airborne weapons included the AT-2 Swatter, first seen aboard surface vehicles, and the SA-7 Grail, more usually a shoulder-fired infantry surface-to-air missile which could be used either as an air-to-air or air-to-ground missile. The SA-7 was noted on some Mil Mi-24A/D gunships, which have also carried the AT-2. Hind-E carried four AT-6 Spirals, while the wire-guided Sagger was adapted to the Mil Mi-2 for training, the Mil Mi-8 and Yugoslav Air Force examples of the Aérospatiale Gazelle.

Unfortunately for tacticians eager for a showpiece confrontation between tanks and helicopters, the major conflict of the early eighties was one in which armor played no part – the Falklands War of 1982. Helicopters, however, were in the front line as usual,

Top: The Mil Mi-12 failed to enter production, but was intended to exploit the vast Soviet wastes in the search for scarce resources.

Above: Sikorsky's S-75 makes extensive use of composite materials and may yet lead to a production helicopter of similar design.

Opposite top: Mil's mighty Mi-26, the world's largest production rotorcraft.

Opposite: Sea King helicopters and Sea Harrier VSTOL fighters both played key roles in the Falklands War of 1982, flying from HMS *Hermes*.

Inset opposite: With no roads in the Falklands, Wessex helicopters provided much-needed mobility.

HUGHES AH-64 APACHE

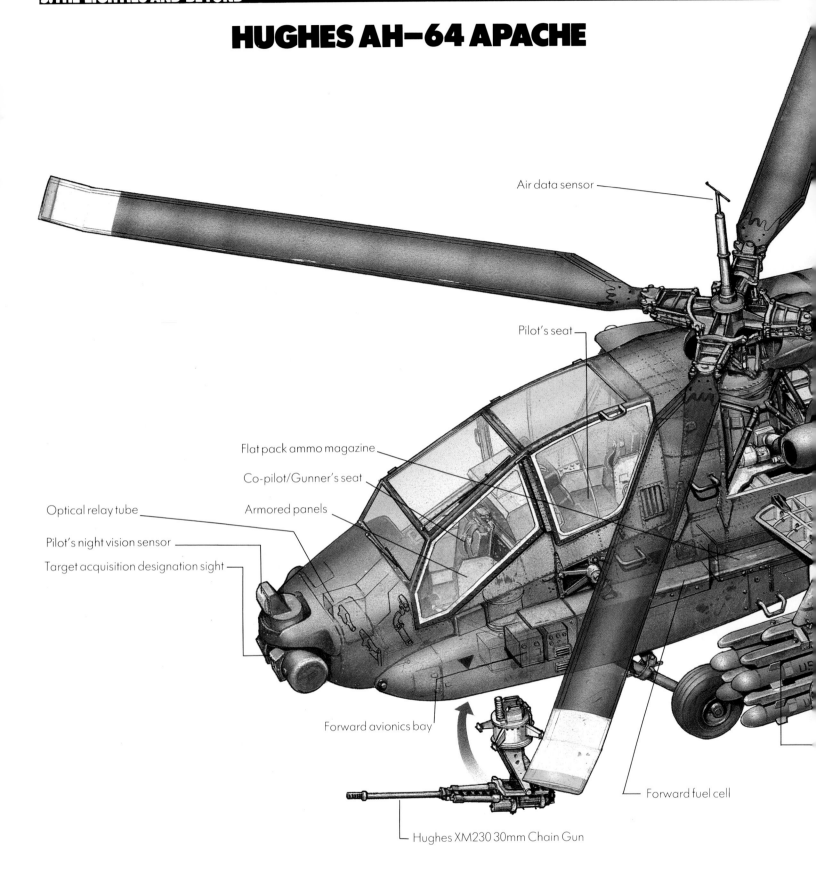

Air data sensor

Pilot's seat

Flat pack ammo magazine

Co-pilot/Gunner's seat

Optical relay tube

Armored panels

Pilot's night vision sensor

Target acquisition designation sight

Forward avionics bay

Forward fuel cell

Hughes XM230 30mm Chain Gun

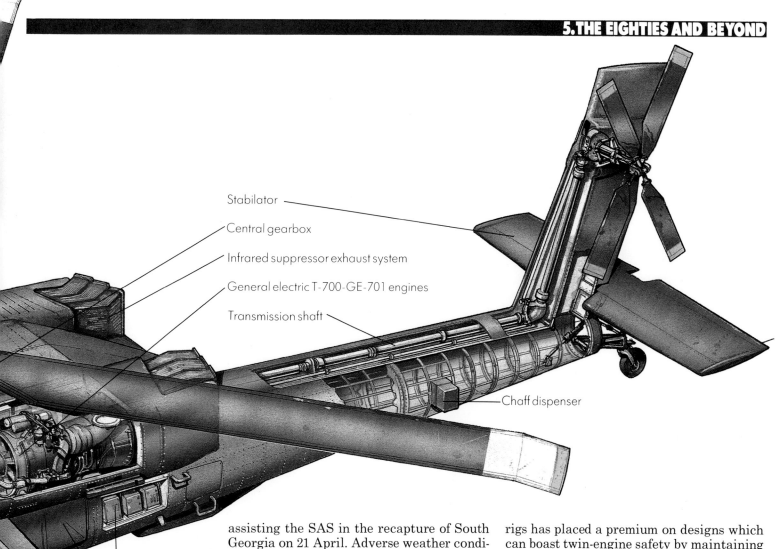

Stabilator

Central gearbox

Infrared suppressor exhaust system

General electric T-700-GE-701 engines

Transmission shaft

Chaff dispenser

Aft avionics bay

Aft fuel tank

Stub wing construction

2.75 inch rocket launcher pod

Hellfire missile launcher

assisting the SAS in the recapture of South Georgia on 21 April. Adverse weather conditions caused two machines to crash in a blizzard, but 13 troops and four crew were rescued by a single Westland Wessex before further lives could be endangered. Thenceforth, helicopters played a vital role in overcoming inhospitable terrain and maintaining ship-shore communications, the machines used ranging from the diminutive Westland Scout to the Boeing Vertol Chinook heavy lifter.

Spinoffs from the military rotorcraft world have become more numerous in recent years, providing the civilian sphere with unexpected benefits. The infra-red scanner common in modern weapons systems packages, for example, was linked with a computer by Bristow Helicopters of the UK to assist air-sea rescue attempts in bad weather and visibility. It is claimed that the device can pick up a target in the water as small as a single human head. Airborne lasers, meanwhile, have been adapted from their usual missile guidance role in the search for mineral deposits in the North American mountains. By analyzing differences in the reflections of the laser from the mountainside at which it was directed, the system proved a time-saving survey tool that confirmed the helicopter as a prime instrument in the continuing search for new resources in inaccessible and inhospitable terrain.

The search for oil and gas has also significantly increased the importance of the helicopter. Operating in support of offshore rigs has placed a premium on designs which can boast twin-engine safety by maintaining height on one, the ability to remain afloat after ditching (either by means of an amphibious hull or flotation buoys), good payload and range and the ability to operate in Instrument Flight Rules conditions, preferably with a single pilot.

Significantly, it is the civilianized versions of proven military workhorses that have provided the backbone of many oil support fleets. Twin-engined developments of the Bell UH-1, Sikorsky's S-61N and Boeing's Civil Chinook have been among the most successful of these, with a strong mid-eighties challenge being mounted by Aérospatiale's Super Puma; the civilianized S-70C version of the Black Hawk seems an inevitable future contender in the field.

In the heavy lift category, the Mil Mi-6 was finally eclipsed as the world's largest production helicopter. Predictably its conqueror came from the same stable – the Mil Mi-26 Halo. A large-ish Mi-6 spin-off, the Mi-10 flying crane, had been produced in limited numbers in the sixties, while the Mi-10K (a short-legged version with a rear-facing chin cabin for ease of winching) progressed no further than the experimental stage. The first type to challenge the Mi-6 had been the Mi-12 which, first flown on 10 July 1968, became the largest helicopter in the world with a length of 37 meters. Initial signs were promising: a maximum payload record – 88,635 pounds (40,205 kg), equal to some 500 men – backed up Soviet claims that the type would help exploit the natural gas and oil resources believed to exist in the roadless, railless wastes of northern and western Siberia. But the giant twin-rotor craft, reminiscent of a Short Belfast freighter with wingtip rotors, encountered development problems and faded from the scene. The West's only response was the three-engined Sikorsky S-65A previously detailed, with an all-up weight higher than any previous Western rotorcraft. The first civil versions had yet to appear by the mid eighties, however.

With East and West having tried and seemingly abandoned the skycrane concept in the sixties, it took a pioneer from an earlier decade still – Frank N. Piasecki of tandem-rotor fame – to resurrect it. But his Heli-Stat had several important differences, the most striking of which was a large airship-like gasbag. This was supported by four girder-frame outriggers, each with a Sikorsky S-58 attached. The helicopter components – which were intended to support the payload, the airship section lifting the ensemble's empty weight – had linked controls, the pilot of the port aft S-58 having overall control of the craft.

Piasecki's intention was to combine the helicopter's precision hovering capability with the lifting capacity of the airship – payload in this case was 52,000 pounds, just 3000 pounds less than the Heli-Stat's empty weight. Two shipping containers could be accommodated between the girder frame elements, but it was the ability to carry large, underslung loads that persuaded the US Forest Service to place the type's first order before its maiden flight scheduled for sometime in the mid eighties.

The only pure helicopter to approach the Heli-Stat's size since the abandonment of Boeing Vertol's experimental XCH-62 was the previously mentioned Mil Mi-26. Though its rotor diameter was smaller than that of the Mi-6 or Mi-10, eight blades were needed to bear aloft a leviathan whose payload and cargo hold approximated to that of the Lockheed C-130 Hercules transport aircraft. Significant weight savings over its predecessors had been achieved (among them a titanium rotor hub) so that the helicopter's empty weight did not exceed half of the permitted maximum take-off figure. To emphasize its capabilities, the Mi-26 established five payload-to-height records in February 1982: on 3 February, for example, test pilot G. F. Alfeurov eclipsed the records of the Sikorsky S-64 and Mi-12 by lifting payloads of 10,000 and 25,000 kg to heights of 20,997 ft and 13,451 ft respectively. The final record saw the Mi-26 attain a height of 2000 meters with an all-up weight of no less than 125,153 pounds – a total akin to the weight of a Boeing 737 airliner. In normal service, a figure of 44,100 pounds would be more usual, equivalent to perhaps 100 troops. It was hoped that the Mi-26 would open up the Siberian swamp and tundra regions as the ill-fated Mi-12 had been intended to do, and for this reason steel-spar rotor blades and other conventionally reliable materials were used in design rather than the composites favored by Western manufacturers. There was, however, enough of note in the Mi-26's design to emphasise that Mikhail Mil's bureau continued to provide the Soviet armed forces with an enviable rotary-wing tactical transport capability – whatever civilian use might be made of its products.

The helicopter's relative complexity compared with its fixed-wing counterparts had tended to result in high empty weights and, as a consequence, reduced payloads. The replacement of piston by turbine engines had obviously been a great step in the right direction. The major comparable breakthrough sought in the eighties was the replacement of as much metal as possible by lightweight composite structures. Aérospatiale had made the early running with their new generation of light- and medium-size helicopters, but even greater savings were demanded by a US Army project that saw the two US giants, Sikorsky and Bell, as the main rivals. The objective of the Advanced Composite Airframe Program (ACAP) was to achieve weight and cost savings of 22 and 17 percent respectively compared with metal airframes, with added advantages including enhanced maintainability and reduced radar signature. Minimum requirements of crashworthiness and resistance to attack were, however, insisted upon. The two contenders were the Sikorsky S-75 and Bell's Model D292, both of which relied heavily on the systems of the existing S-76 and Model 222 respectively in order to minimize expense. Rotor systems, too, offered opportunities for simplification and, in some cases, significant weight savings: the rotor head and gearbox of the mighty Mil Mi-6, for example, weighed in at 7055 pounds – more than both its engines!

Aérospatiale made no heavyweight claims for their Starflex rotor hinge that replaced three conventional hinges with a single balljoint, but the potential savings in maintenance costs were obvious. Also in the maintenance field, some helicopters adopted airtight blade spars filled with nitrogen under pressure; by lowering the pressure, any cracks or holes would operate a visual indicator to alert groundcrew. A similar method, known as the Integrated Spar Inspection Method, utilized a vacuum in place of the gas.

The problem of bearing lubrication had been eased by the development of elastomeric (metal and rubber laminate) bearings which required no oil. Aérospatiale in particular were instrumental in simplifying the necessary hinges at the rotor head. The shape of rotor blades had changed, too, with those of helicopters such as the MBB/Bolkow Bö 105 having swept-back tips to

enable the speed of sound to be approached more closely by the rotating blades.

Sikorsky tested a new system with their S-69, announced in early 1972 and first flown on 26 July 1973. The Advancing Blade Concept (ABC) resulted from the theory that if two co-axial counter-rotating rigid rotors were employed, then the aerodynamic lift created by the advancing blade would be fully utilized without the penalty imposed by the flapping of the retreating blade. In other words, no lift need be created by the retreating blade since the dissymetry would cancel itself out with the twin-rotor layout. Blades were as rigid as possible, and flapping minimal. With more thrust generated, higher speeds would be possible. Tests saw the XH-59A, as it was designated, attain speeds of up to 303 mph and ceilings of 25,500 feet without the addition of fixed wings – a unique achievement. Neither was the helicopter's behavior in low-speed or hovering flight affected by its high-speed capabilities. Sikorsky re-worked the XH-59A to incorporate a ducted pusher propeller as research continued into the mid eighties, when it was still possible that the concept might be used for a new generation attack helicopter.

Although the Kamov Ka-32 Helix was first revealed to the West at Minsk Airport in 1981, when a flying crane version was exhibited, the type's origins were clearly not of the eighties. The inevitable shipboard anti-submarine version, since designated Ka-27, was intended to replace the venerable Ka-25, yet its larger fuselage suggested that the type could now fulfil a dual role in the manner of the Sikorsky/Westland Sea King/Commando series as an infantry assault transport and vertical replenishment provider for ships at sea. It was to become a familiar sight on the helicopter platforms

of the newer Soviet ASW guided missile cruisers in the early eighties.

Another Soviet update announced in 1981 had been the Mi-17, which appeared at the Paris Air Show and was an amalgamation of the sixties-vintage Mi-8 airframe with the 1900 shp Isotov turboshafts of the Mi-8's naval ASW derivative, the Mi-14 Haze. The Mi-14 had made its maiden flight in 1973 and entered service four years later, differing from its progenitor in possessing a watertight hull in which the appropriate anti-submarine equipment was installed: the whole bore some resemblance to the Sikorsky S-61/SH-3 series. It had been a surprise that it had taken the Soviets so long to spin off such a derivative from a type that had first appeared in 1961; whatever the reason for the delay, the Soviet Naval Aviation's shore-based ASW capability was dramatically upgraded by its acqustion, replacing as it did the venerable, piston-engined Mi-4 Hound. Despite Haze's advent, the Kamov Ka-25 had continued in its shipboard role by virtue of its compact size.

Elsewhere in the Warsaw Pact, the Polish PZL concern drew heavily on its experience of license-production of the Mil Mi-2 to design the original W-3 Sokol. First flown on 16 November 1979, it employed two Polish-built Glushenkov turboshafts, each developing 870 hp, to transport 12 passengers. It did not seem beyond the realms of possibility that the type might be marketed in the United States, where the Mi-2 was already being offered.

With worldwide emphasis in the eighties being on utility and multi-purpose machines to enable the purchaser to buy more for his money, it was something of a surprise to find a British private-venture helicopter trainer, the Robinson R22, doing such good

Above: The Advancing Blade Concept pioneered by Sikorsky with their S-69 promised high speeds and attractive flight characteristics. Research continued into the eighties.

Above: The Westland W.30 employed tried and tested Lynx systems in a larger design with considerable potential for civil and military applications.

Right: The Mil Mi-14 Haze was a belated anti-submarine variant of the Mi-8 that replaced the Mi-4 with land-based Soviet ASW units.

business. A diminutive two-seat machine, it was claimed in 1984 to be the world's fastest-selling piston-engined helicopter.

The market for hard wearing, hard working utility machines continued to grow apace – a situation that encouraged Bell to re-commence production of their single-turbine Model 205, the veteran UH-1 Huey of Vietnam fame. Development of the basic design had taken its descendants so far upmarket, in the shape of the Models 412 and 214 ST, that manufacturers such as Westland had been able to undercut them with more basic designs.

Westland's pitch for a share of this market took the shape of the Westland W.30, which combined the proven rotor, transmission, hydraulic and electric systems of the Lynx with twin turboshafts (Rolls Royce Gem 60 or General Electric CT7) and a 19 passenger/5,800 pound payload cabin. A further development, the W.30-404 with composite advanced-geometry five-blade rotor, crashworthy structure and automatic flight control capability, was competing in the mid eighties for the RAF's AST404 requirement for a Wessex/Puma support helicopter replacement. Other competitors were the Black Hawk and the Super Puma.

Having previously achieved success in the civil helicopter market with derivatives of military designs, Sikorsky announced in 1975 their intention of claiming a larger share of commercial sales in the eighties with a purpose-built design, the S-76 Spirit. As if to prove that military and civil objectives could not be separated quite that easily, the type made use of a scaled-down version of the UH-60A's rotor system, as well as benefiting from Black Hawk development work.

From the first flight of the 12-passenger second prototype on 13 March 1977, it was clear that Sikorsky had a winner. The following six years saw 530 orders placed, not only from civilian operators but from such disparate sources as the Icelandic Coast Guard, Malay Air Regiment and the Philippine and Jordanian air forces. Among the machines ordered for the latter two services included a number configured as air ambulances. The S-76's two 650 shp Allison turboshafts gave the type an impressive performance in all climates and conditions, including a top speed of 178 mph, and it was perhaps predictable that a developed military variant, the AUH-76 (as the company styled it, in imitation of the US Armed Forces' Attack/Utility Helicopter designation), would be touted in 1984 as a 'poor man's Black Hawk'.

This, however, was typical of the prevailing trend that was to carry through into the early eighties; the specialized types of yesteryear were being replaced by a new breed of utility helicopter which could take combat, corporate and commuter duties equally in its stride.

International collaboration continued to increase. Having joined forces with Aérospatiale to good effect, Westland forged a new link with Agusta of Italy to design and market the medium transport/utility EH.101, too late to compete for the AST404 prize but similar in capability. As if to emphasize the overlap in the frequently quoted categories of modern rotorcraft, the three-turbine EH.101 also threatened the territory of the long-serving and hitherto unchallenged Boeing Vertol Chinook at the lower end of the heavy lift field. In terms of existing types, it was similar to the Sikorsky S-61 (which both collaborators had manufactured for some years), the upper limit on size being imposed by the Royal Navy ships from which the Sea King operated since the EH.101 was to be offered as a possible replacement. Westland's production of the Sea King had by this time standardized on the Commando assault transport and the radar-equipped AEW variant for shipborne use.

A stranger geographical mix resulted in

Above: Unveiled in 1981 the Ka-32, will continue Kamov's monopoly of Soviet shipborne anti-submarine helicopters into the next century. The pictured civilian prototype was taken to new world records by test pilots Zuyeva and Yeremina.

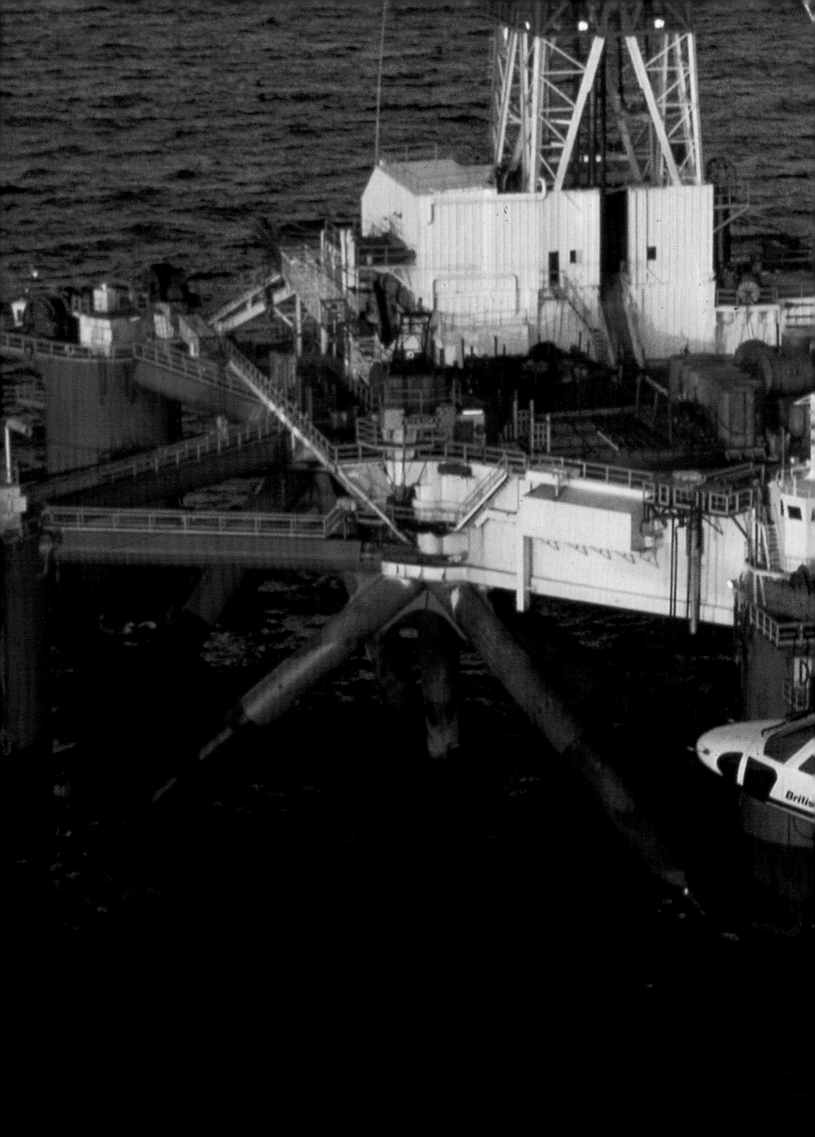

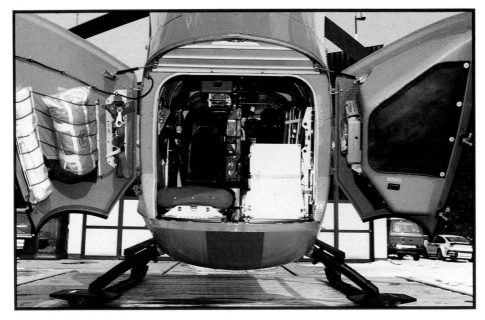

Above: The clamshell rear doors of the BK 117, a joint Japanese/German venture, make it unique among civil helicopters of the 1980s.

Above right: The unmanned Gyrodyne DASH system provided the US Navy with anti-submarine capability for some years.

Previous page: The Sikorsky S-76 Spirit was intended specifically for the civil market, and sales have endorsed the type's design concepts. Its twin engines make it particularly suitable for oilfield support missions.

Germany's Messerschmitt-Bölkow-Blohm teaming with Kawasaki in Japan to shape the civil BK 117, a multi-purpose twin turbo-shaft helicopter which clearly benefited from the many years of Bö 105 research carried out by the German firm. The Bö 105's famous rigid rotor assembly was used for the new product, which boasted clamshell rear loading doors, a rarity on a helicopter of this size. A production line in Indonesia as well as the two originating countries made this arguably the most global of all rotorcraft collaborations. The Germans looked nearer to home, across the border to France this time, for a partner to help design and manufacture a contender for the next generation of European anti-tank helicopter. With the German PAH-2 and French HAC-1 specifications being almost interchangeable, it seemed a natural move for MBB and Aérospatiale to pool their resources and join Westland, Agusta, Bell and Hughes as competitors in a remarkably crowded field.

The only wholly new purpose-built European gunship to emerge in hardware form in the early eighties was the Agusta A.129 Mangusta twin-engined attack helicopter, first flown on 15 September 1983 and already scheduled at that time to enter Italian Army service in 1986. Its development was obviously assisted by Agusta's success with their A.109, and there were certain similarities between the types. The A.129's rotor system was noteworthy in making use of glassfiber spar and composite skin – a combination which not only saved weight but could boast tolerance at high levels against hits from 12.7 mm ammunition. Being a latecomer on the gunship scene, it was designed to be able to accept eight Hughes TOW, eight HOT or six Hellfire anti-tank missiles on stub-wing attachment points – and, although systems and avionics were not, perhaps, as complex as those of the AH-64A, the twin Rolls-Royce Gem-powered A.129 was also a contender for the German Army's

PAH-2 specification for a replacement for the Bö 105.

Back in the United States, Bell were developing several new rotor systems. The first, a bearingless rotor, was tested on a Model 222 executive helicopter and featured a flapping yoke inboard with pitch changes occurring at a point roughly one quarter of the way along each rotor blade. With all major components of the new system being of composite construction, a weight saving of 15 percent was reckoned to have been achieved.

A further Bell innovation was a new anti-torque device, the Ring Fan, developed by senior design engineer H. E. Lemont and announced in September 1981. Somewhat similar in appearance to Sud Aviation's *fenestron* concept, it was claimed to reduce noise and increase speed of sideways flight by up to 50 mph, as well as the evident advantage of providing additional safety by physically encircling the tail rotor. The first Bell design to take advantage of the Ring Fan was the Bell Model 400 Twin-Ranger, revealed in 1983.

Meanwhile Hughes were experimenting under a two year US Army contract with the possibility of dispensing with a tail rotor altogether. They flew an example of the OH-6 on 17 December 1981 with a new, hollow aluminum tail boom manufactured by Aircraft Engineering Corporation of California. The boom was pressurized by a fan, and an air stream venting from a slot along the starboard side of the boom united with the rotor downwash. The whole followed the contour of the tail boom, the resultant forces counteracting the fuselage's natural tendency to rotate in the opposite direction to the main rotor.

Directional control was achieved by means of a puffer vent at the tail, through which more pressurized air was directed in the appropriate direction. Among the advantages of the configuration claimed by Hughes were an increased safety factor on the ground, less noise, fewer aerodynamic inefficiencies and simplicity of maintenance.

One important application of the rotorcraft that seemed likely to increase in future decades was the unmanned drone helicopter. Pioneers of the system were the Gyrodyne Company of America, whose DASH (Drone Anti-Submarine Helicopter) weapons system equipped 90 US ships in 1966. Powered by a 300 hp Boeing T50 shaft turbine and with provision for two homing torpedoes, its radio remote control operated air-drag tip brakes on the contra-rotating twin rotors for directional control.

Future employment of the drone concept is likely to encompass the surveillance rather than the ASW role, with Shorts of Britain only one of many companies testing unmanned reconnaissance drones equipped with camera and sensor equipment for operations over the battlefield. Although the drone concept is not in itself new, with such fixed-wing types as the Ryan AQM-34 Firebee long a part of the US armory, the rotating-wing drone offers improvements in minimizing the size of radar signal, quietness of operation and cost of manufacture that may well take it to the forefront of battlefield reconnaissance techniques in the coming decades.

Vertical take-off aircraft such as the British Aerospace Harrier fighter remain beyond the scope of this book in being fixed-wing aircraft. It should be noted, however, that such tilt-wing research craft of the sixties as the Canadair CL-84 and LTV-

Hiller-Ryan XC-142A had been performing in the helicopter mode when in vertical flight. The Bell X-22A was somewhat different, not only in its ducted propeller configuration but in the fact that it was its power plants rather than the wing itself that were tilted. Bell resurrected this format when commissioned by NASA and the US Army to build two twin-engined tilt rotor research aircraft in collaboration with Boeing Vertol. The difference with the XV-15, which underwent shipboard evaluation trials in the early eighties, was that the diameter of its non-ducted tip-mounted rotors ruled out 'conventional' take-offs and landings although straight and level flight as an aircraft was, of course, possible.

Apart from conventional powered rotor drive, tip-jets have constituted a phenomenon that has remained under periodic consideration for some time. Rarely has the engine itself been intended for rotor mounting, the centrifugal forces of rotation being too strong to permit this. One of the methods considered was to use compressed air, ejected at the blade tips, and it was this that successfully powered the SO.1221 Djinn, Sud Ouest's two-seat agricultural helicopter of the fifties.

The tip jet configuration was also employed by Fairey on the futuristic Rotodyne. Looking rather like a small airliner with stub wings, it was claimed to be the answer to the businessman's perennial plea for fast city-center to city-center transport. In forward flight, the rotor freewheeled like that of an autogiro, two propellers providing the

Below: The shape of things to come? After the pioneering DASH anti-submarine drones of the Sixties, the unmanned rotorcraft has returned to popularity as a possible source of up to date battlefield information. Further developments are anticipated. A Canadair CL-227 is shown.

Bell picked up their experiments with tilting rotors first pursued by the X-22 (*inset left*) when commissioned by NASA and the US Army to build the XV-15 (*main picture*). The XV-15's tip-mounted rotors are of too great a diameter to permit 'conventional' take-offs and landings so these must be accomplished as a helicopter.

means of propulsion as well as yaw (directional) control in slow-speed flight. In January 1959, it set a new closed-circuit helicopter speed record of 190.9 mph, but the project was cancelled in 1962. In many ways, however, the Rotodyne was a project decades ahead of its time, and many subsequent projects from the drawing-boards of the world's rotorcraft manufacturers bore no little relation to this futuristic craft that would seem more at home in eighties skies than those of the fifties. The possibility of a similarly configured 'VTOL feeder-liner' achieving success in future decades cannot be ruled out.

One of the helicopter's major drawbacks has always been its environmentally unacceptable noise level, a subject that has recurred to limit operations from city-center sites. Almost every major city has a heliport to which businessmen may be flown from the nearest out-of-town airport to save the time and trouble of a road journey. In London in 1984, however, the city's sole scheduled rotorcraft service, the Heathrow-Gatwick airport link operated by Sikorsky S-61 helicopters for the British Airports Authority – fell victim to the growing environmental lobby. In a further revealing decision, the go-ahead was given for a dockland STOLport (for short take-off aircraft such as the de Havilland Canada Dash-7) which, it was claimed, would be less noisy in everyday operation than a heliport handling an equivalent number of passengers. Noise was surely a problem which rotorcraft manufacturers ignored at their peril, for it threatened, by default, to remove the grounds for one of the helicopter's long-prized boasts – that of being the most convenient form of air travel yet devised.

Though the military helicopter continued to hold the attention of most observers – and, indeed, inspire a host of improvements and innovations for the benefit of its civilian counterparts – helicopters of the eighties had established many new roles in a workaday world. Whether dispersing oil slicks, deterring drug smugglers, 'topping off' buildings, airlifting lighthouse keepers, taking photographs, inspecting power lines or cleaning factory chimneys, the helicopter had advanced a long way from the days of da Vinci – it had clearly 'risen high' in the aviation firmament.

And, while the Soviet Union's Mil Mi-26 continued that country's obsession with size and weight, myriad smaller types, in many different shapes, sizes and configurations the world over, bore noisy testimony to the fact that the helicopter's future – in both the civil and military spheres – was assured. Just as the pioneers of rotary-wing flight had pooled their expertise and hard-gained knowledge to advance their science, so international collaboration seemed set to provide the design and financial backing for the rotorcraft of the future.

Left: Sud Aviation were early pioneers of the tip-jet method of rotor propulsion with their Djinn agricultural helicopter of the fifties. The system is once more under review in current projects.

Below: The Fairey Rotodyne employed a similar means of spinning the rotor, forward movement being assisted by twin turboprops and a stub wing. Sadly, the project was too far ahead of its time to proceed, but its 'VTOL airliner' concept may yet be vindicated by the shape of future designs.

INDEX

Picture Credits